By Author: Joseph Sumpter
Book Title: Relax and Destress: Flower
Mandalas Pattern Designs Coloring Book For
Stress Relief

Beautiful flower mandalas designs for adults to enjoy coloring for fun and stress relief.

Biography

Joseph Sumpter enjoys working, traveling, and sports

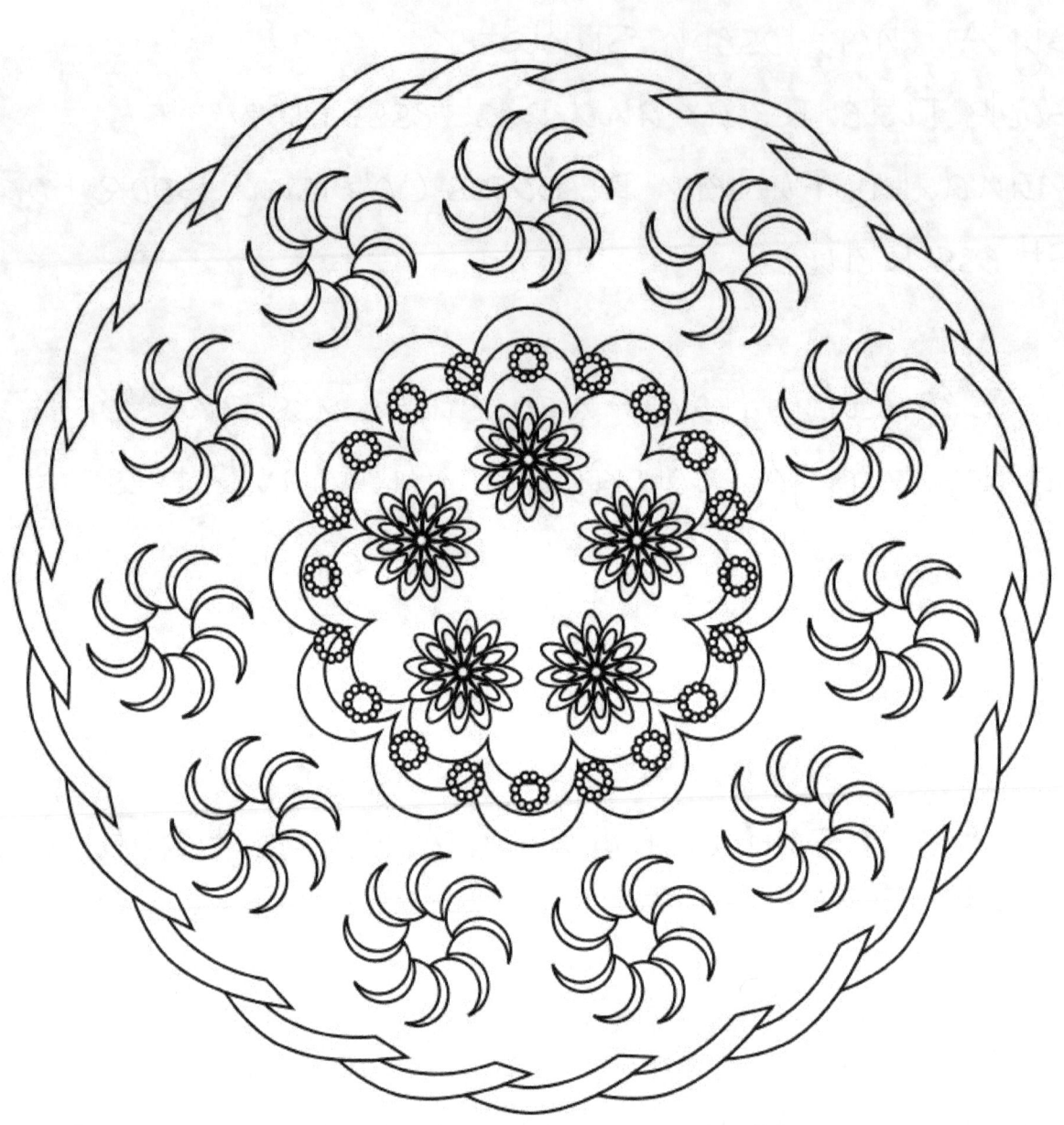

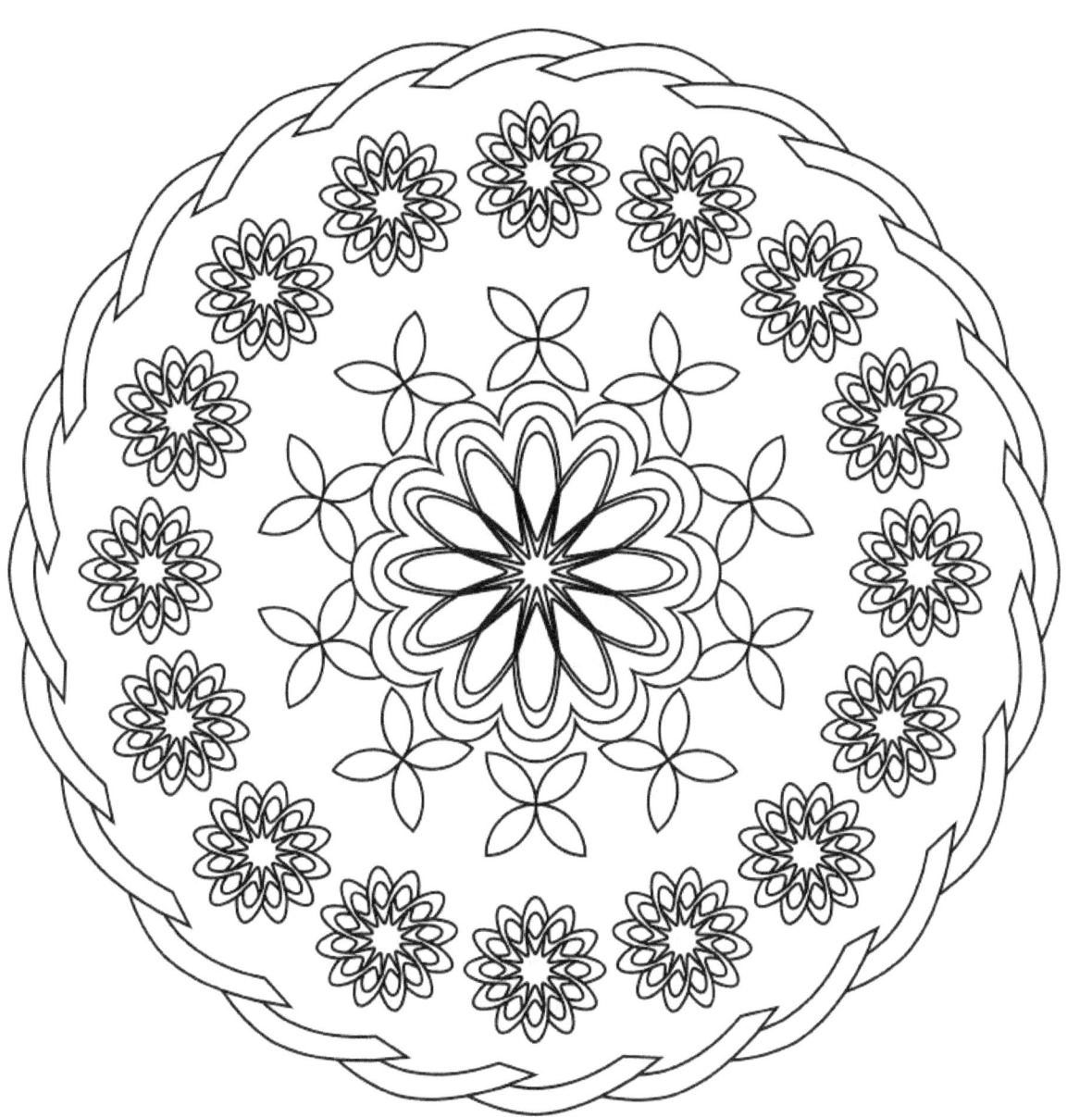

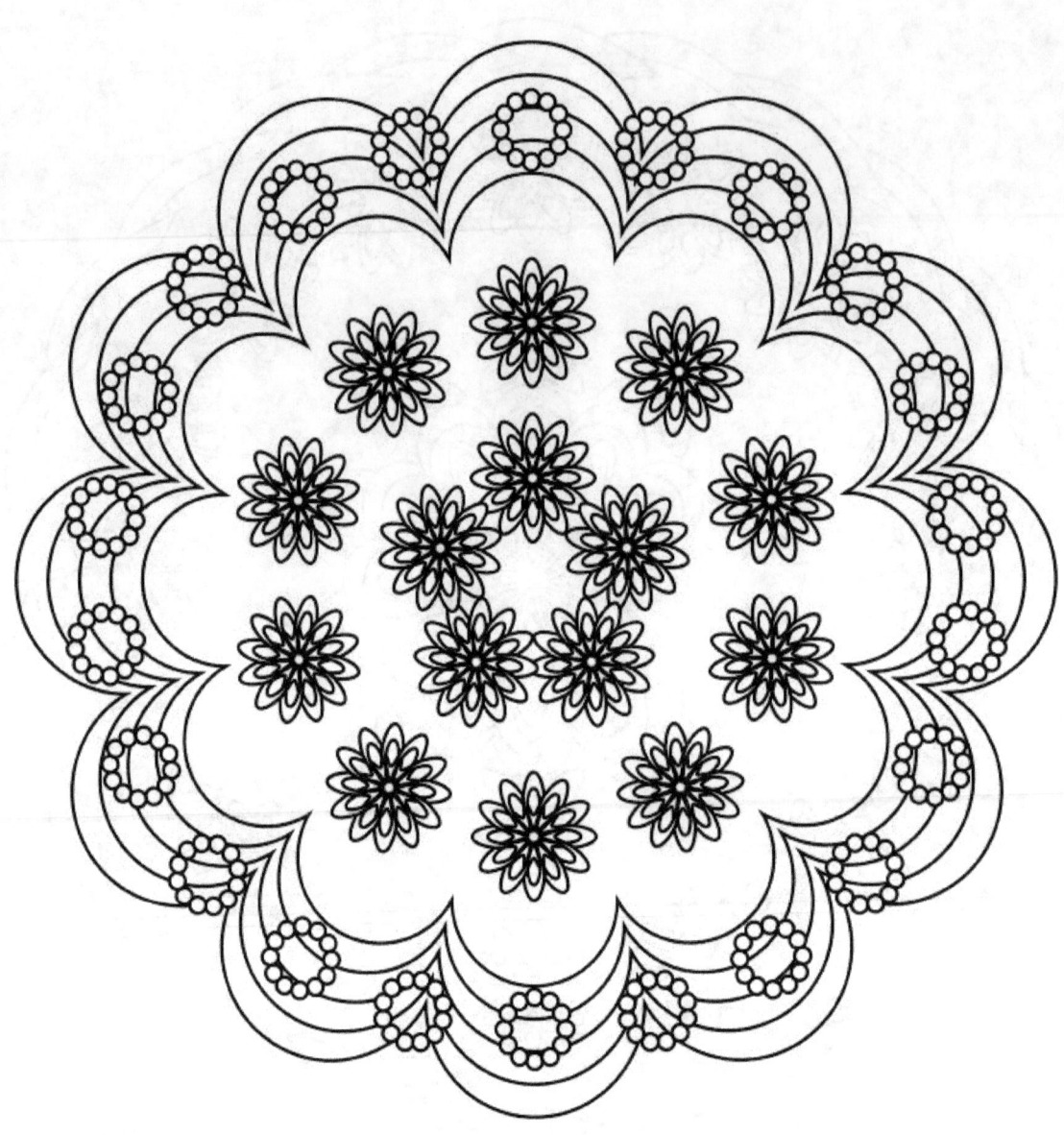

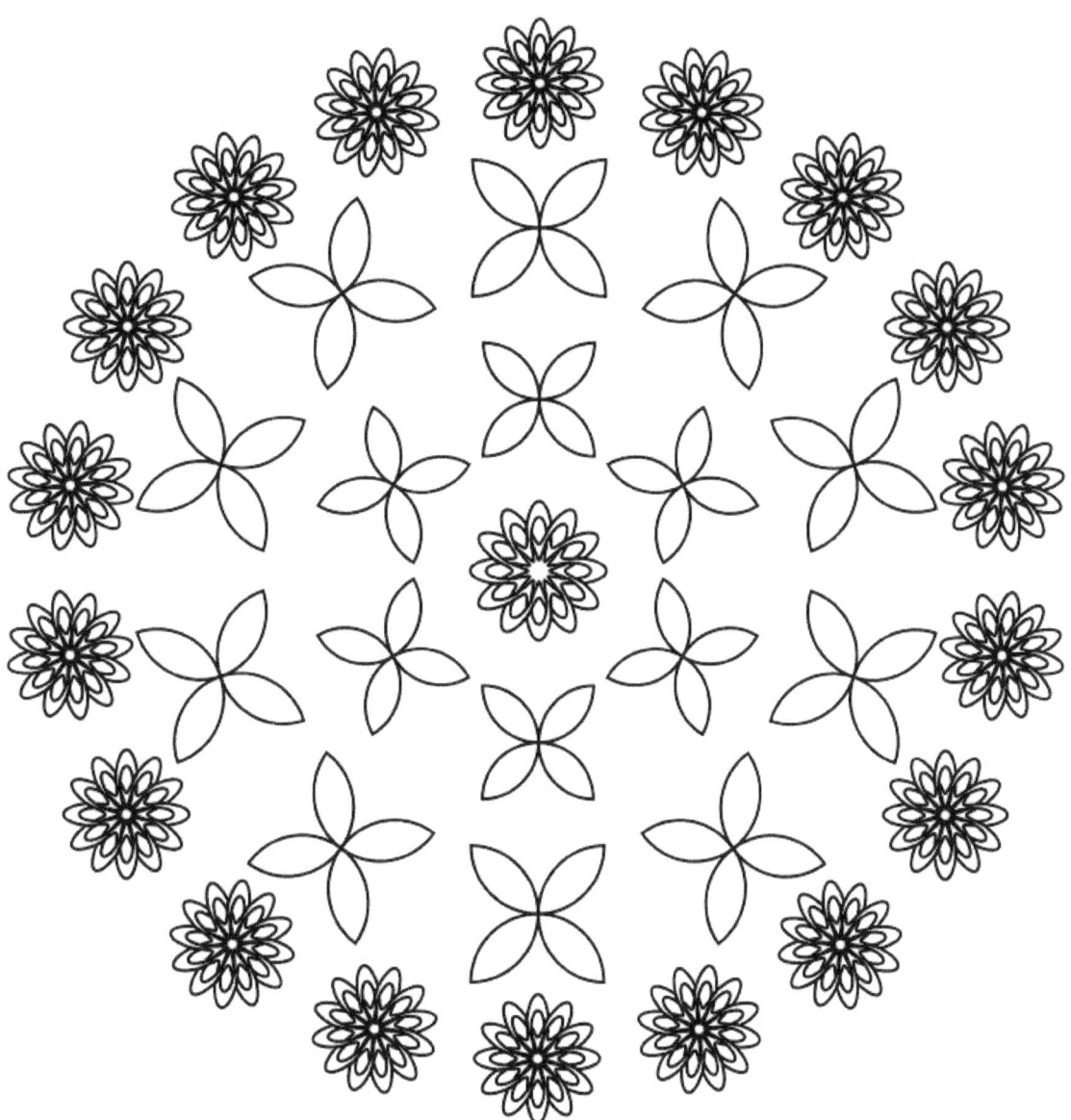

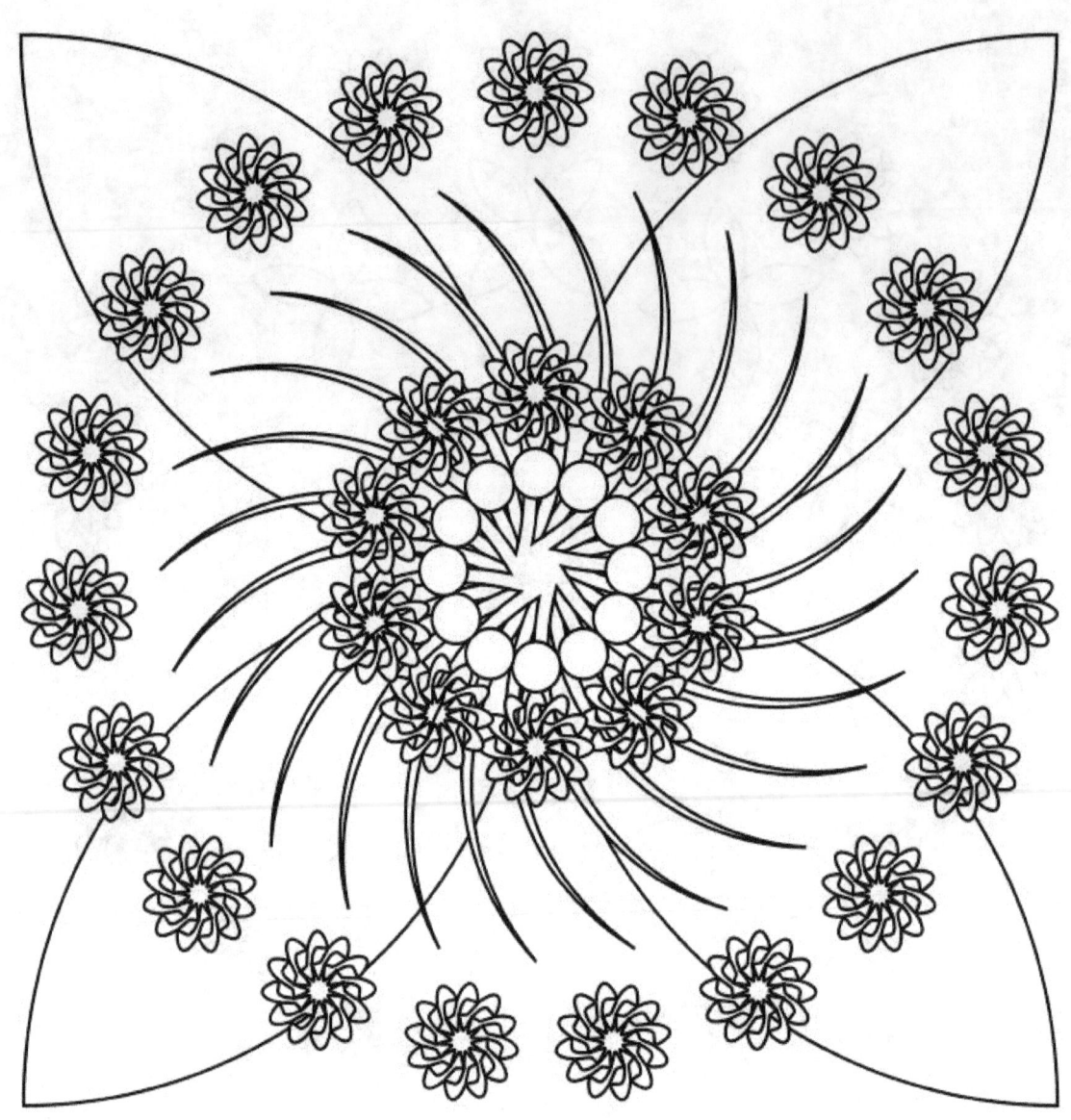

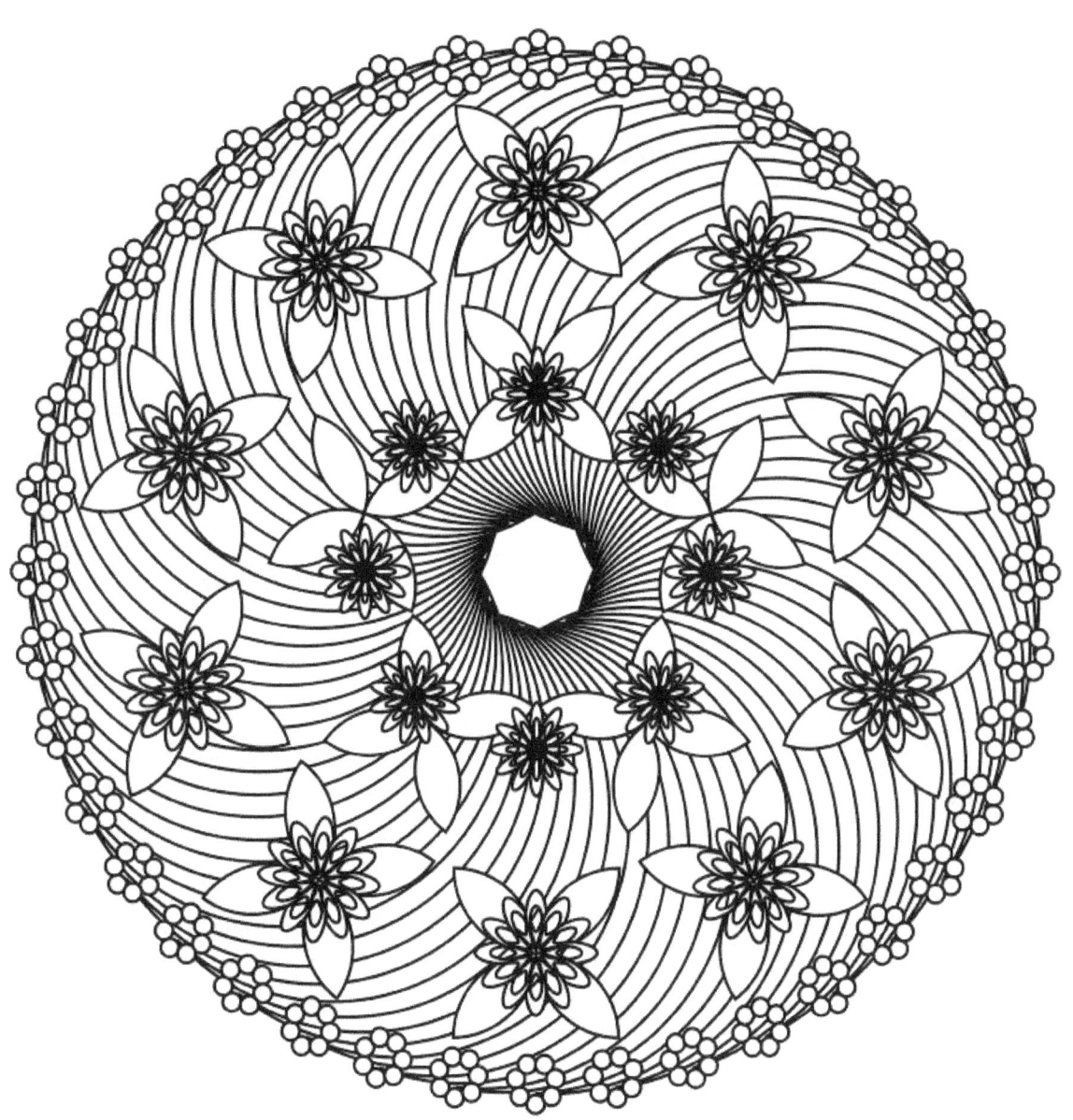

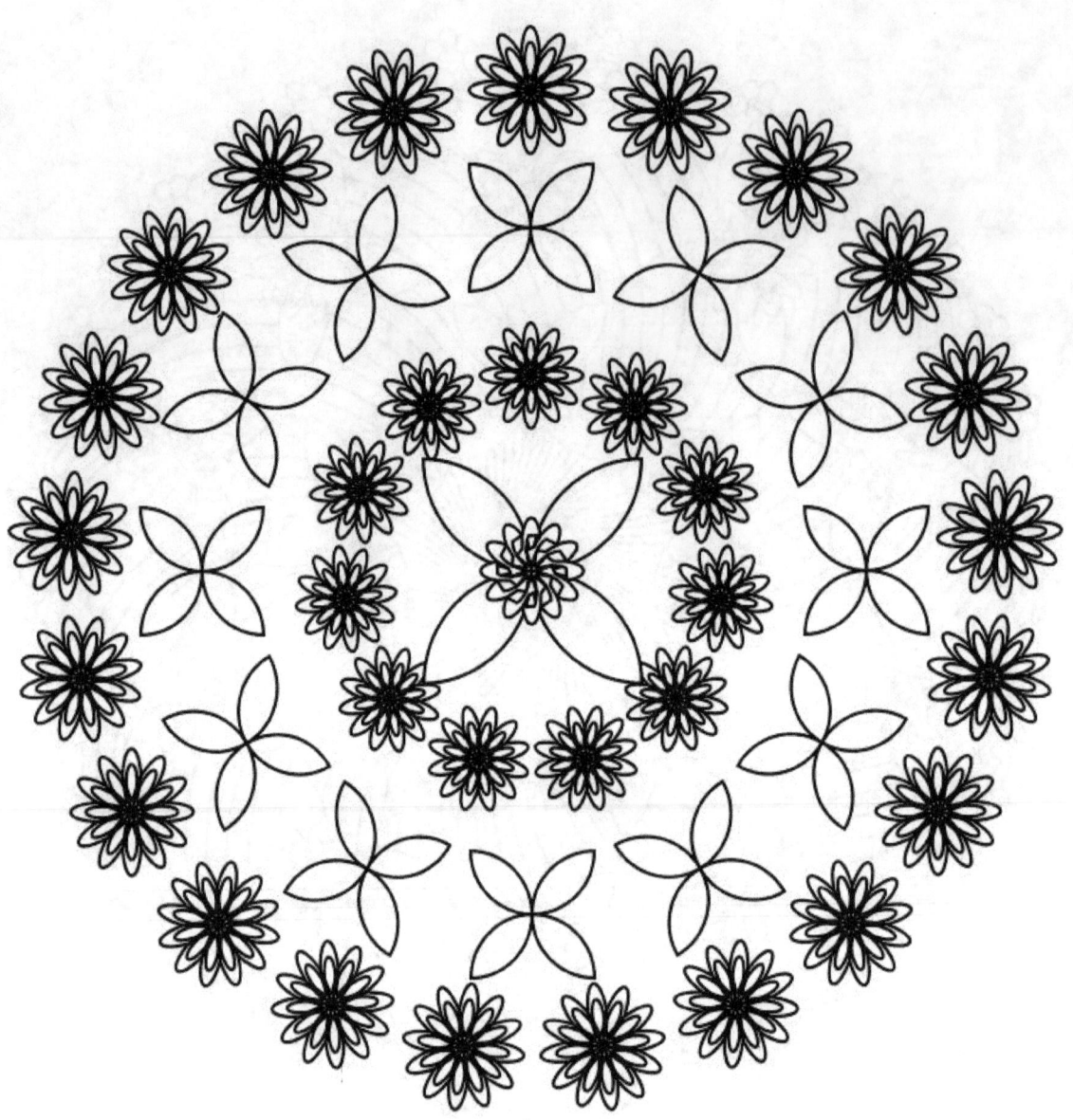

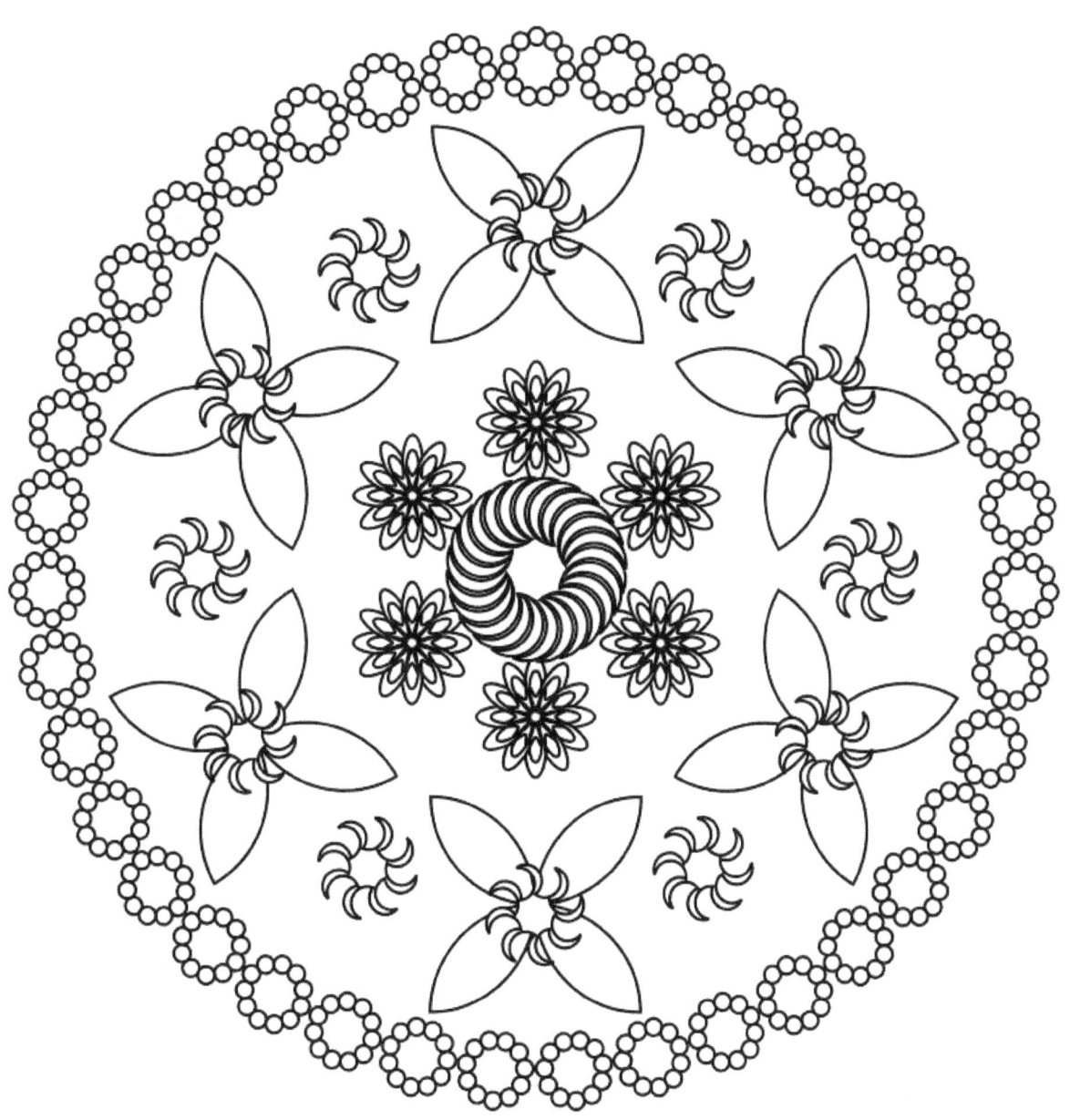

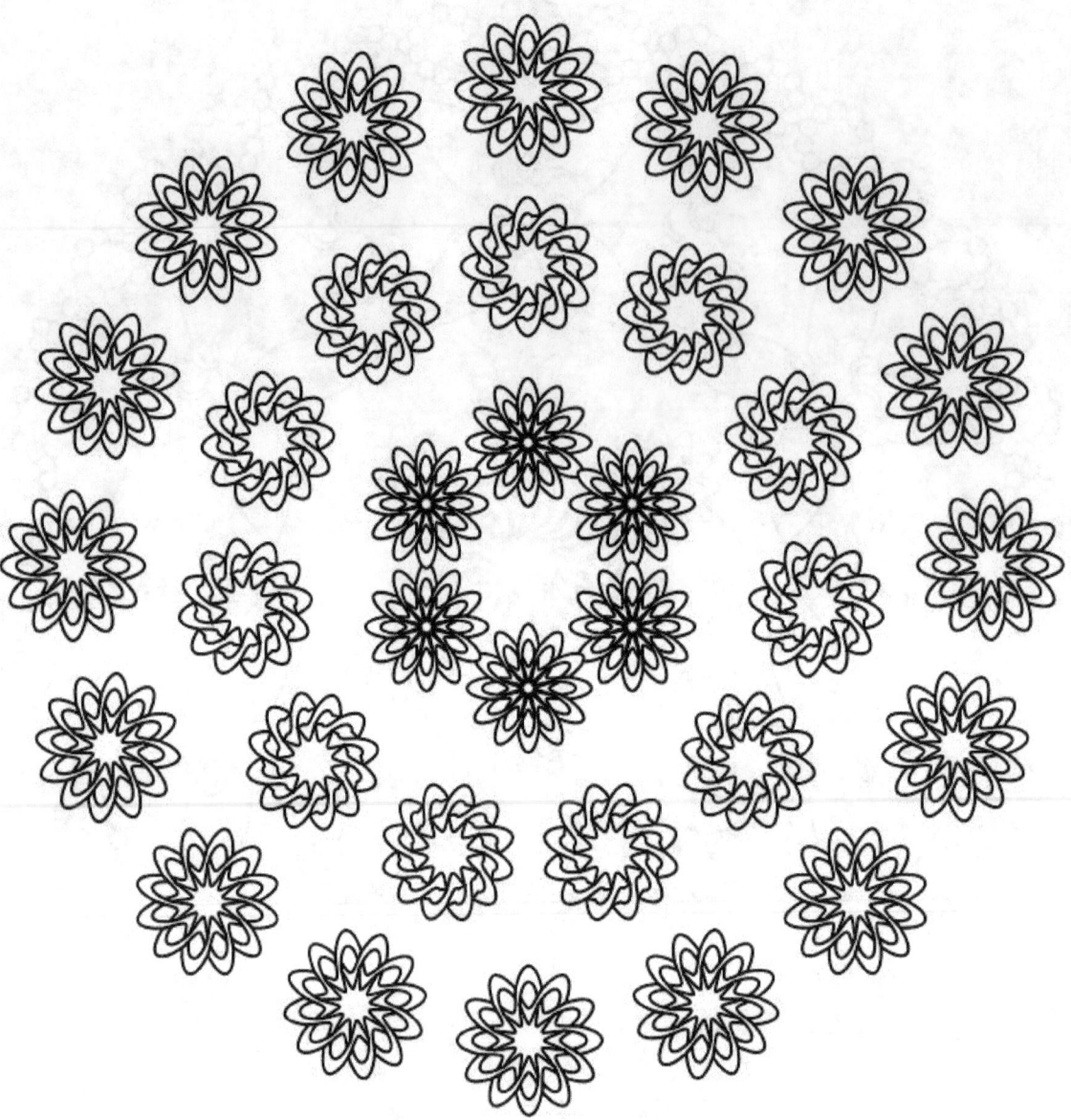

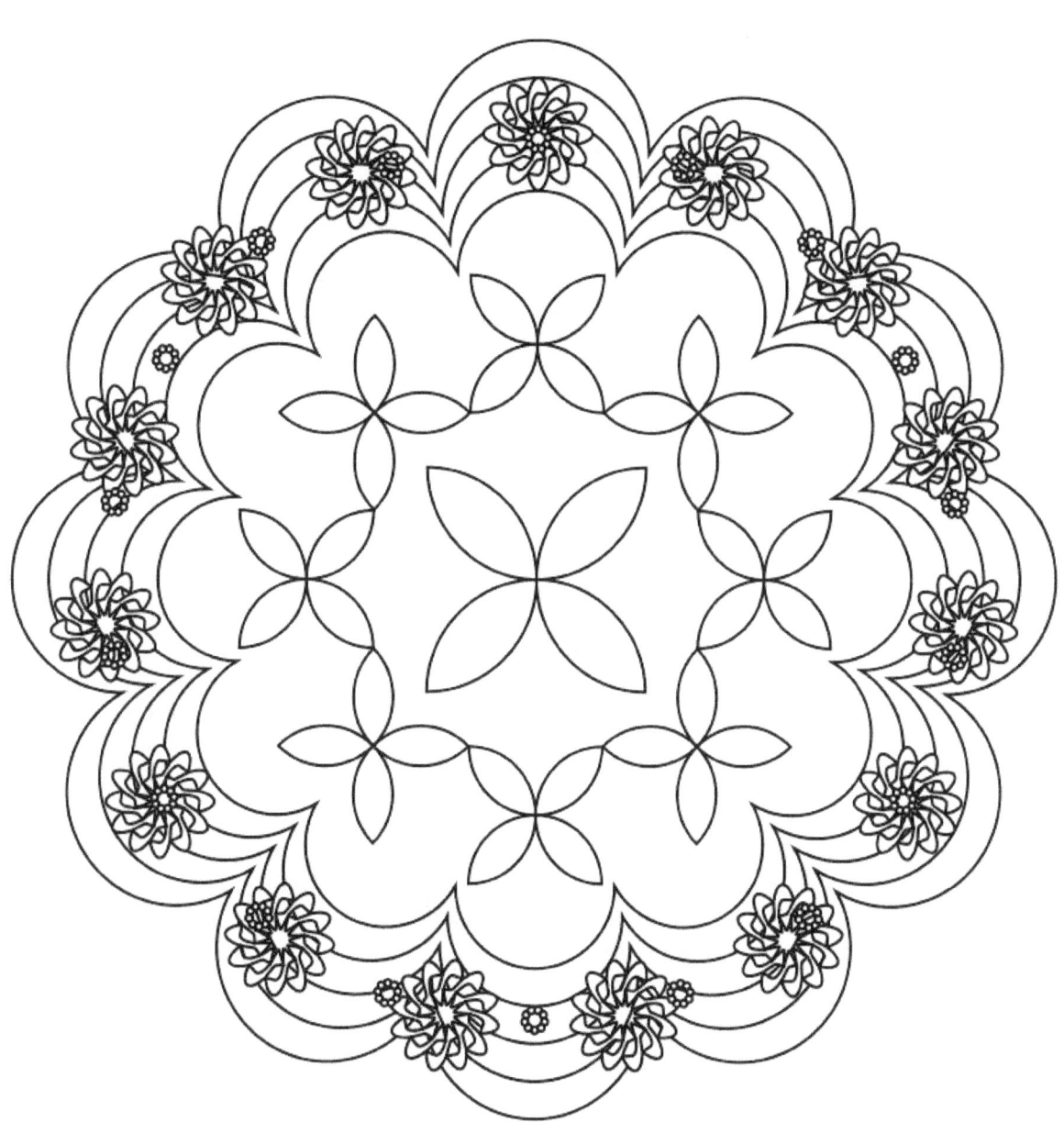

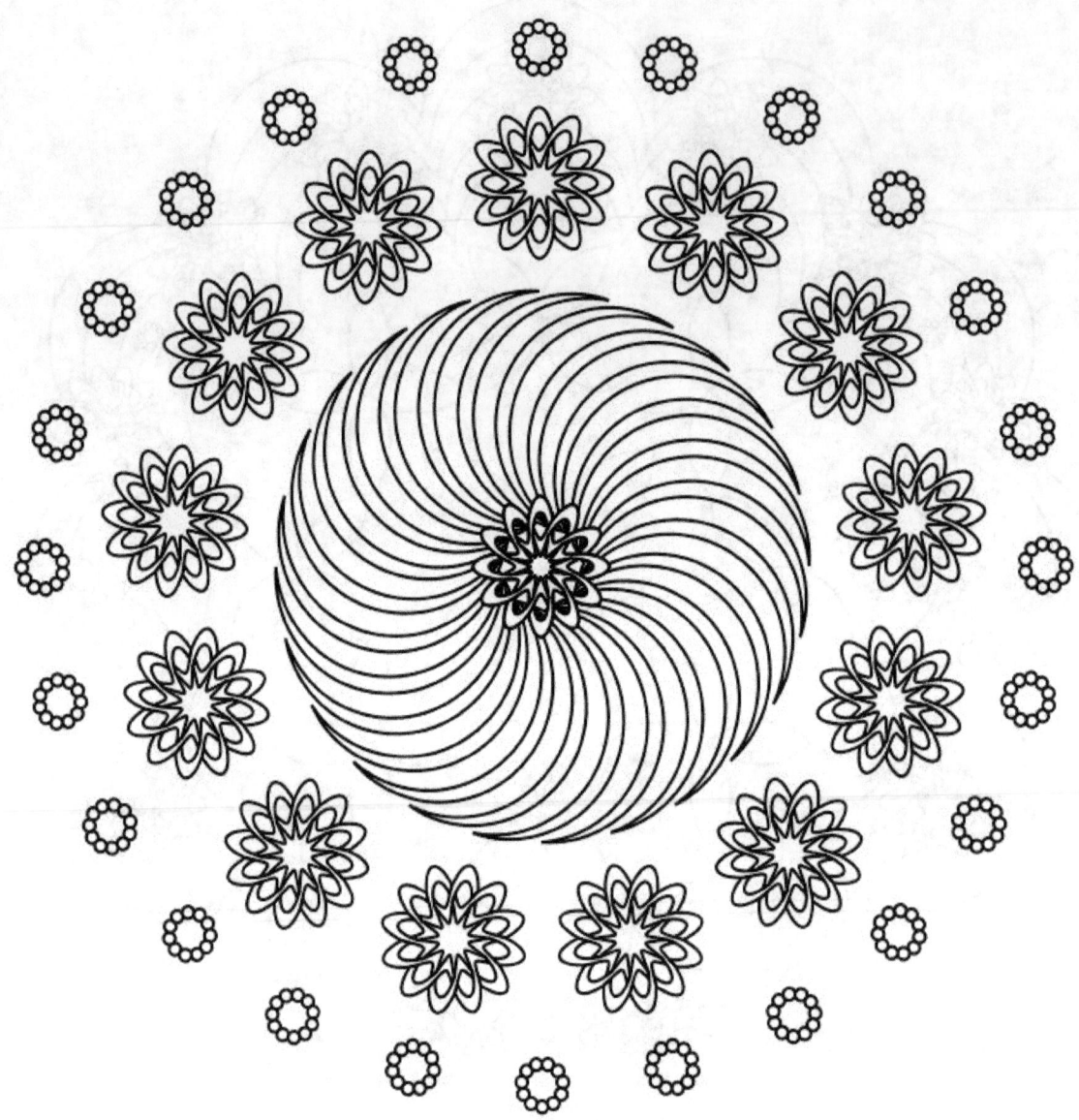

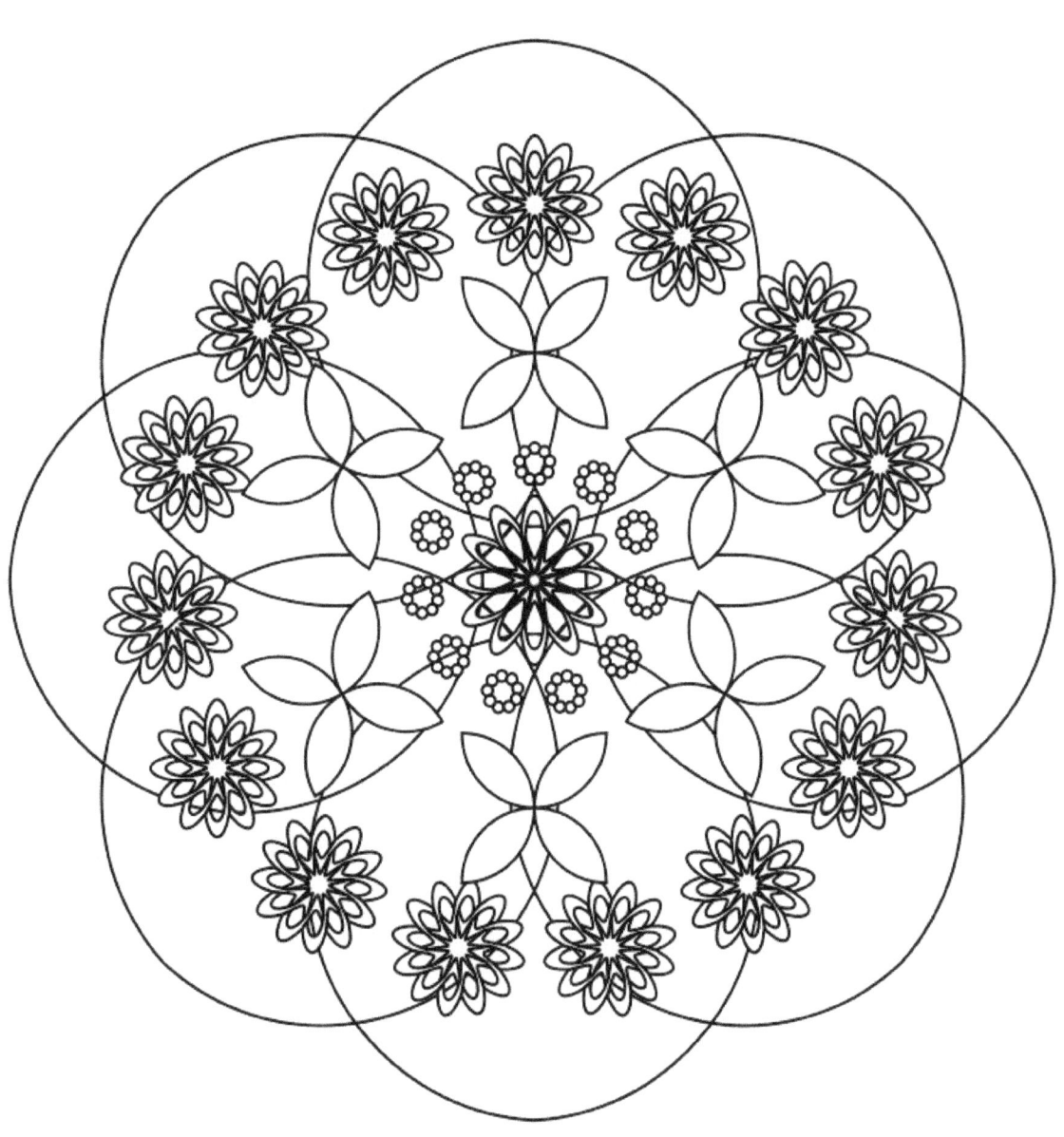

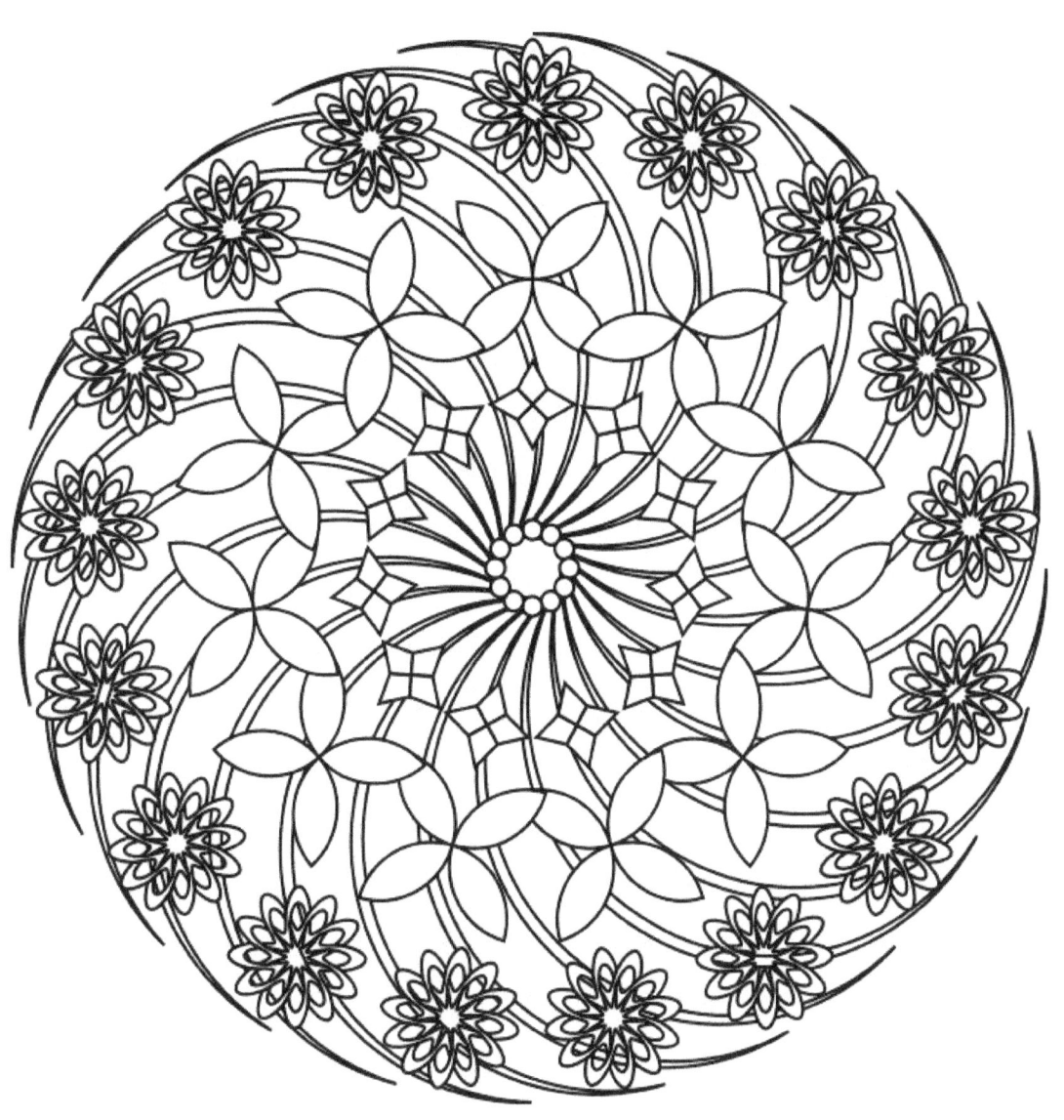

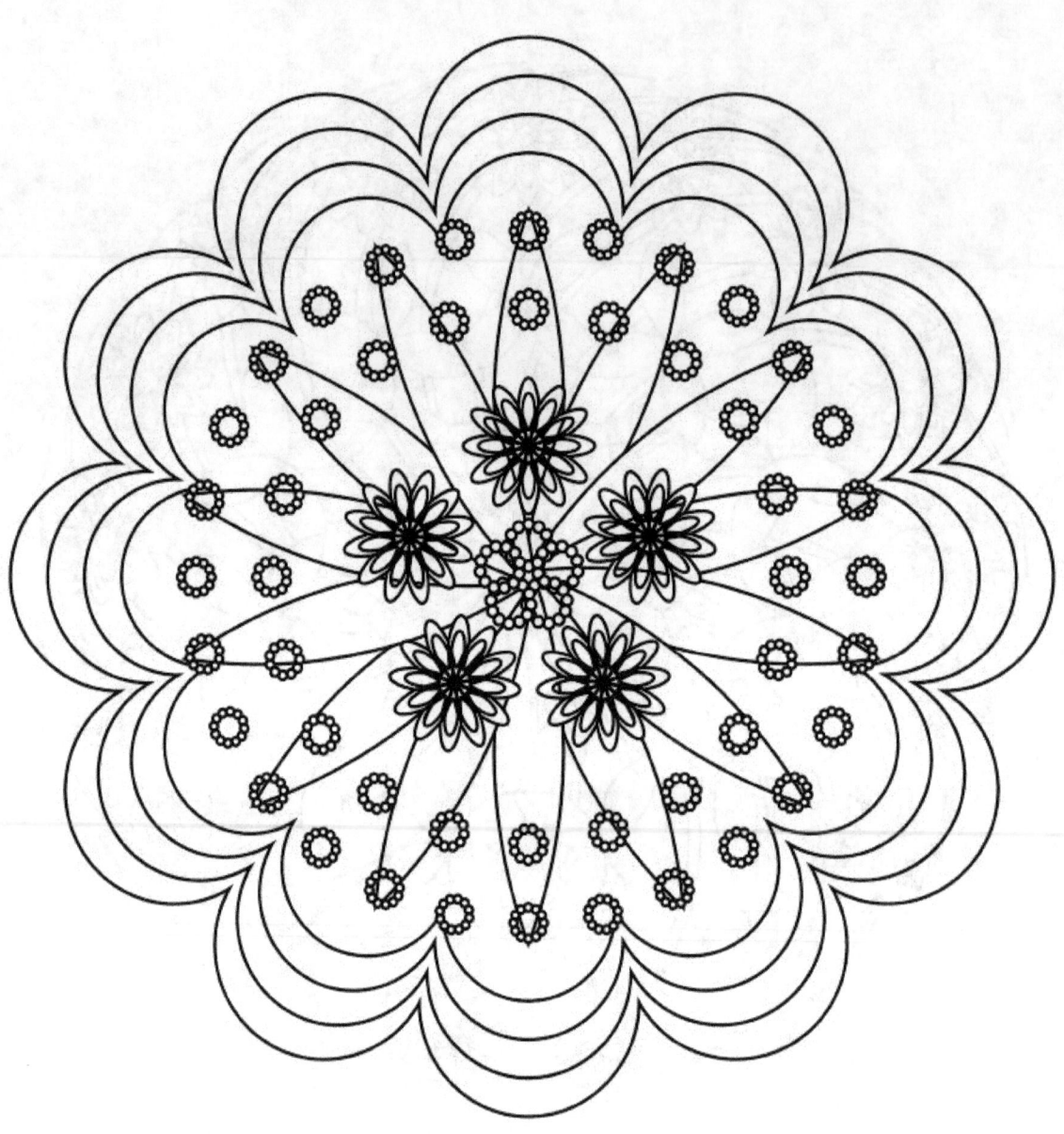

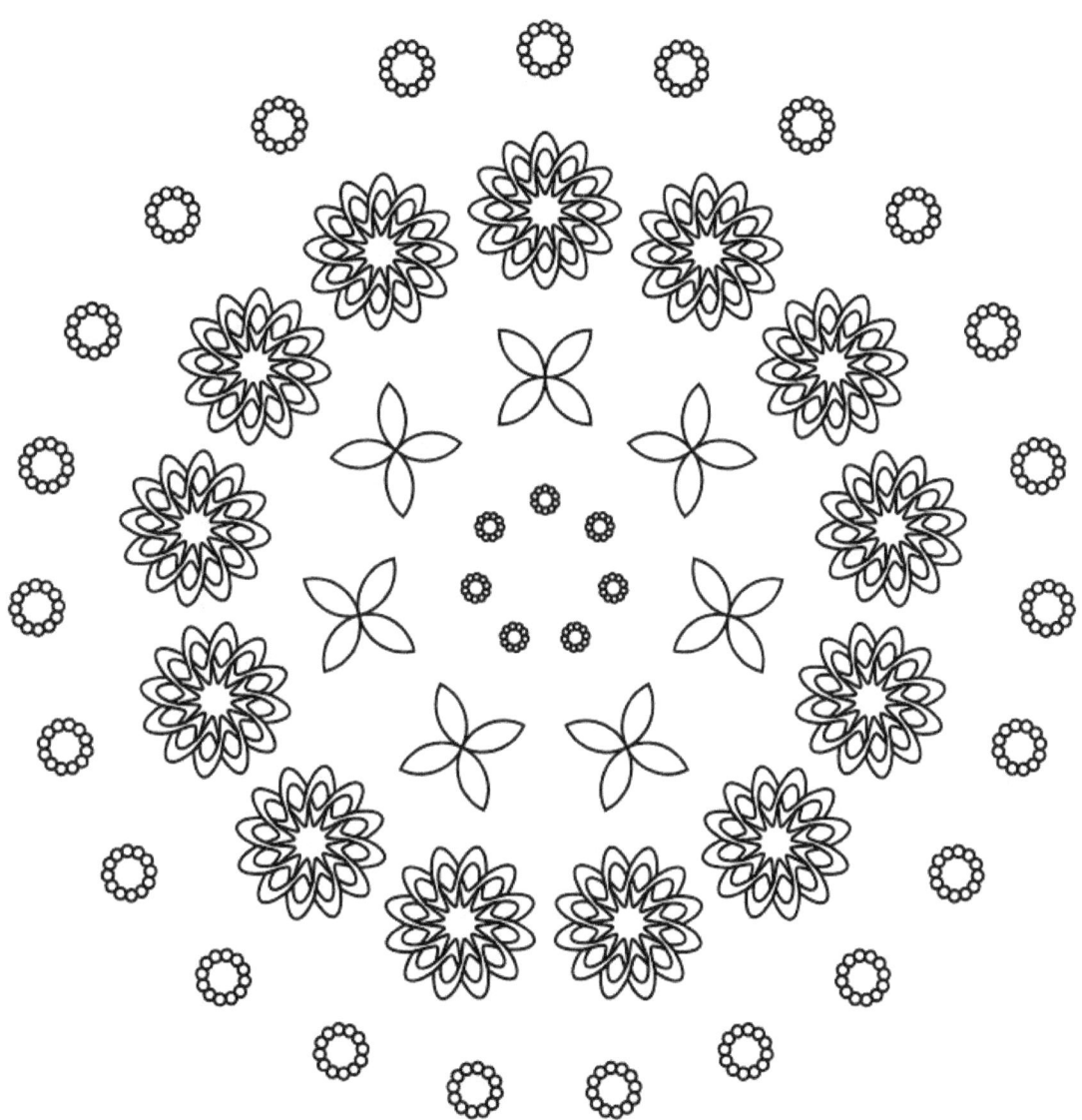

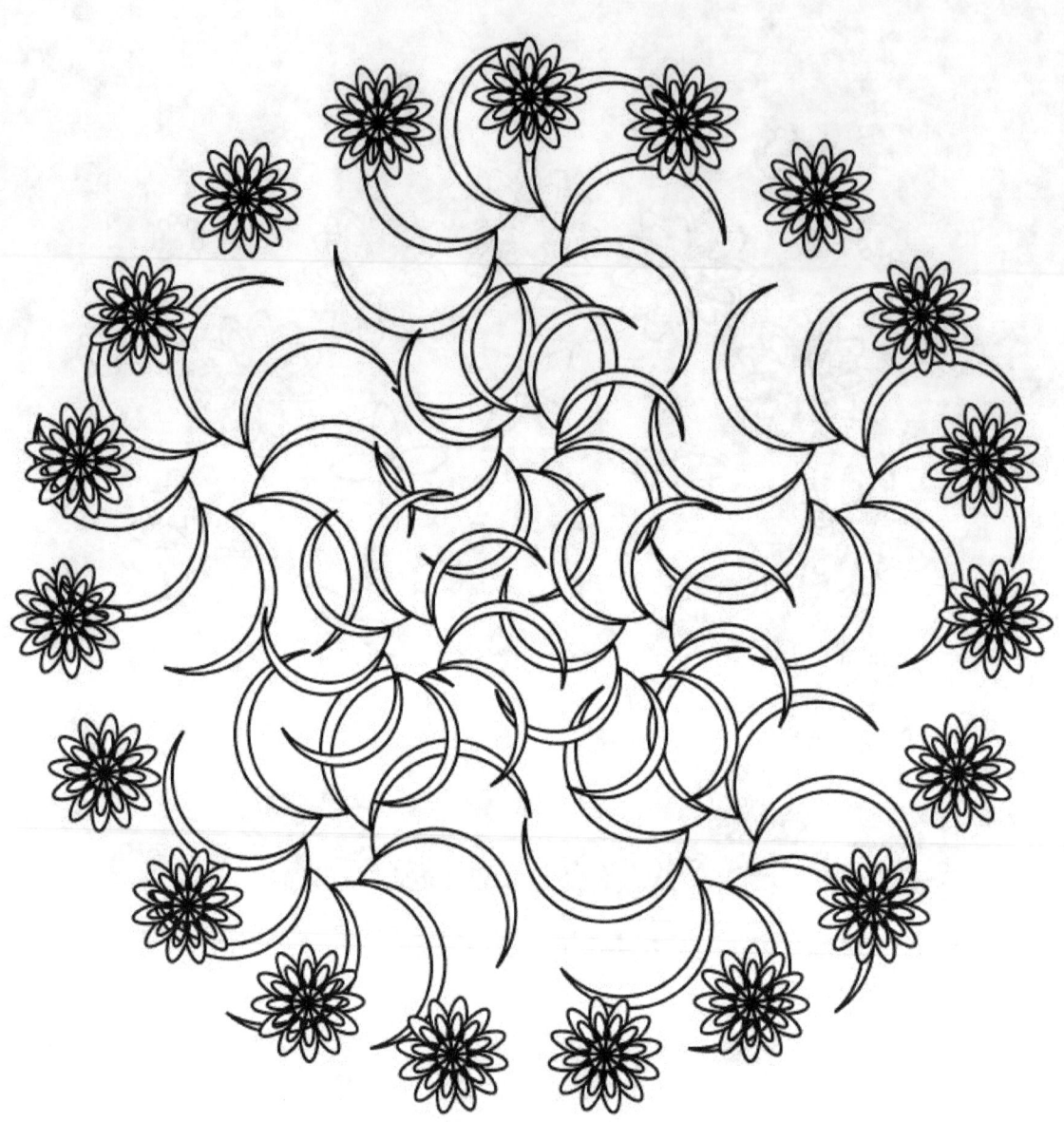

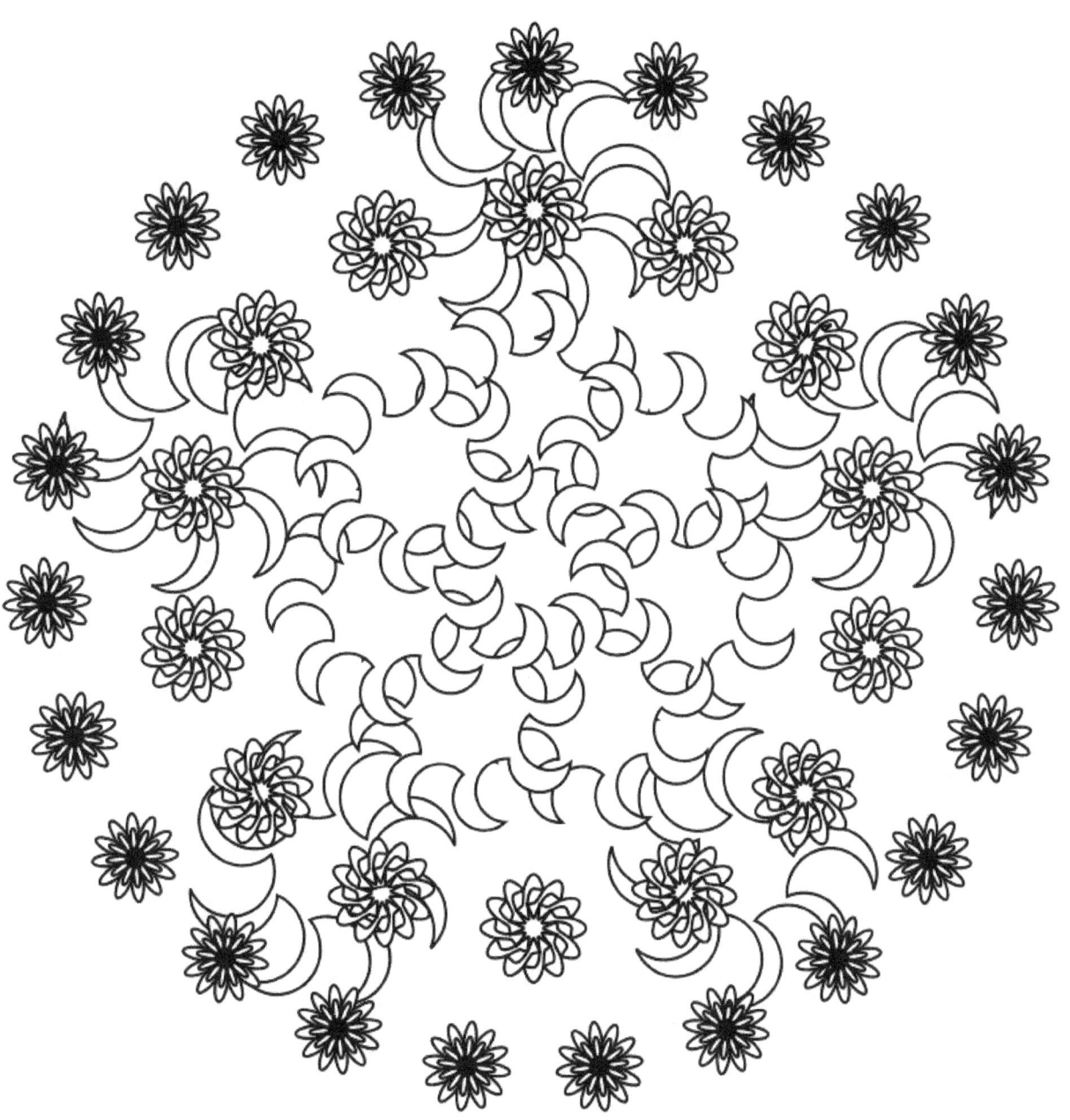

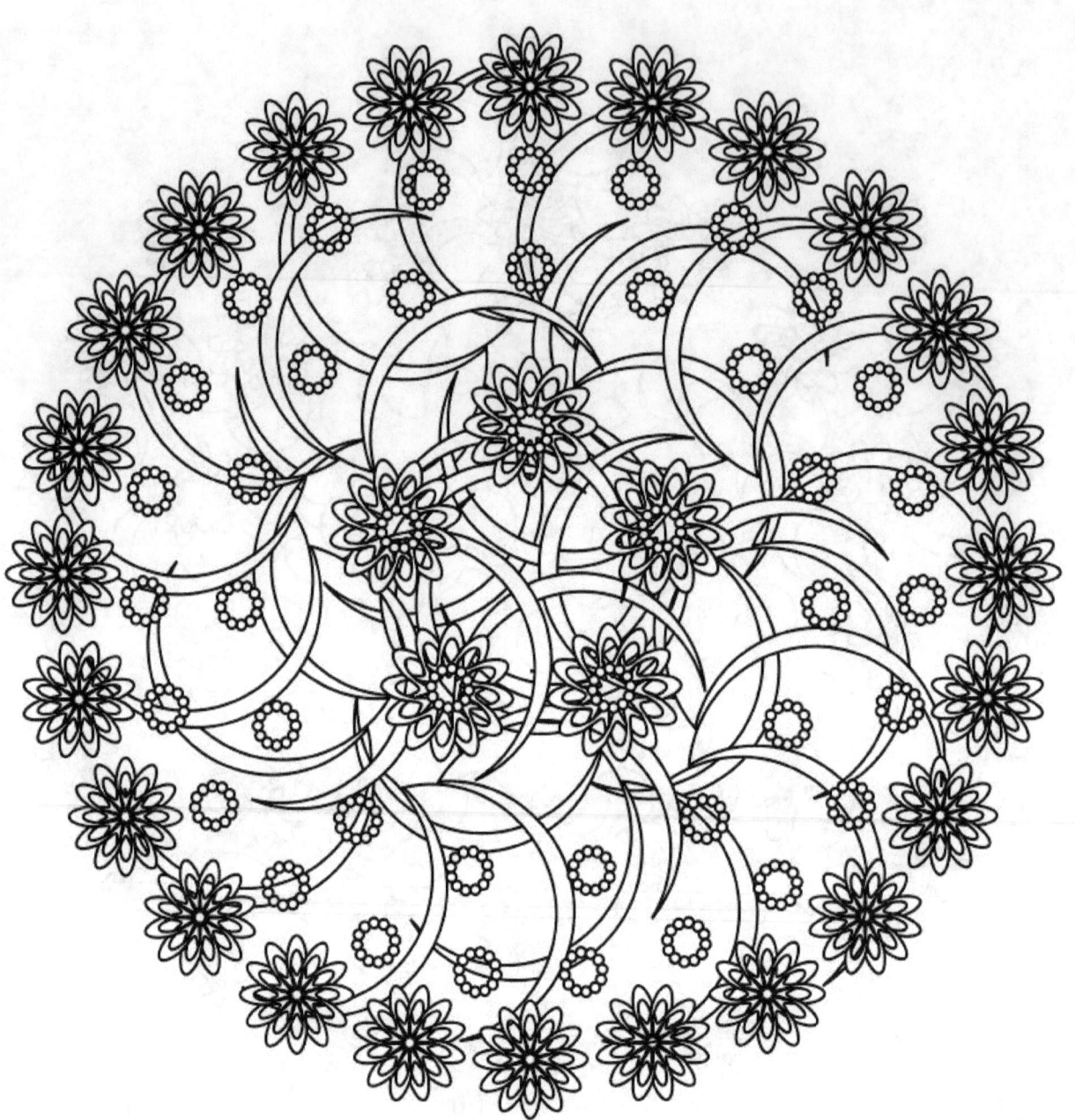

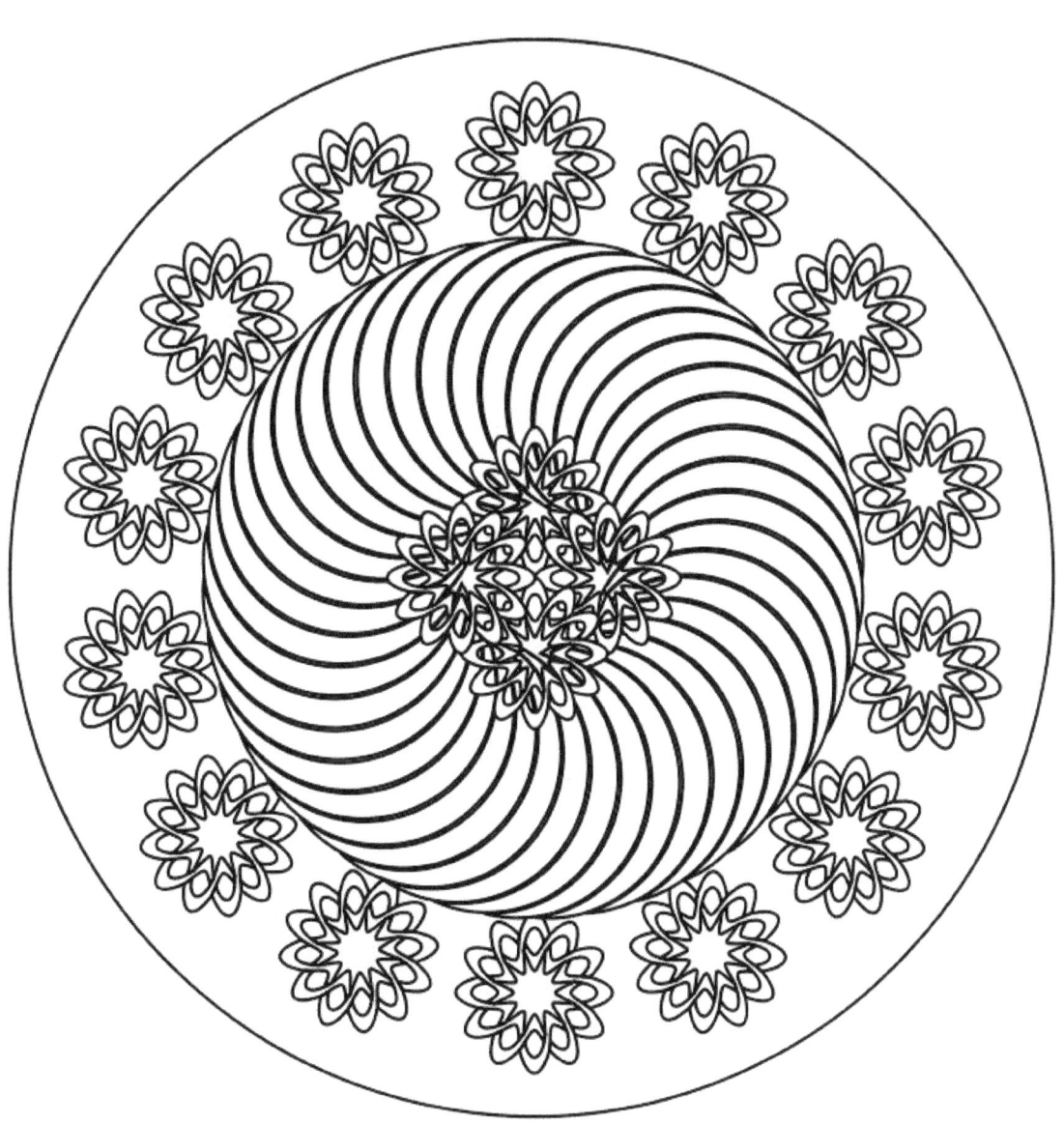

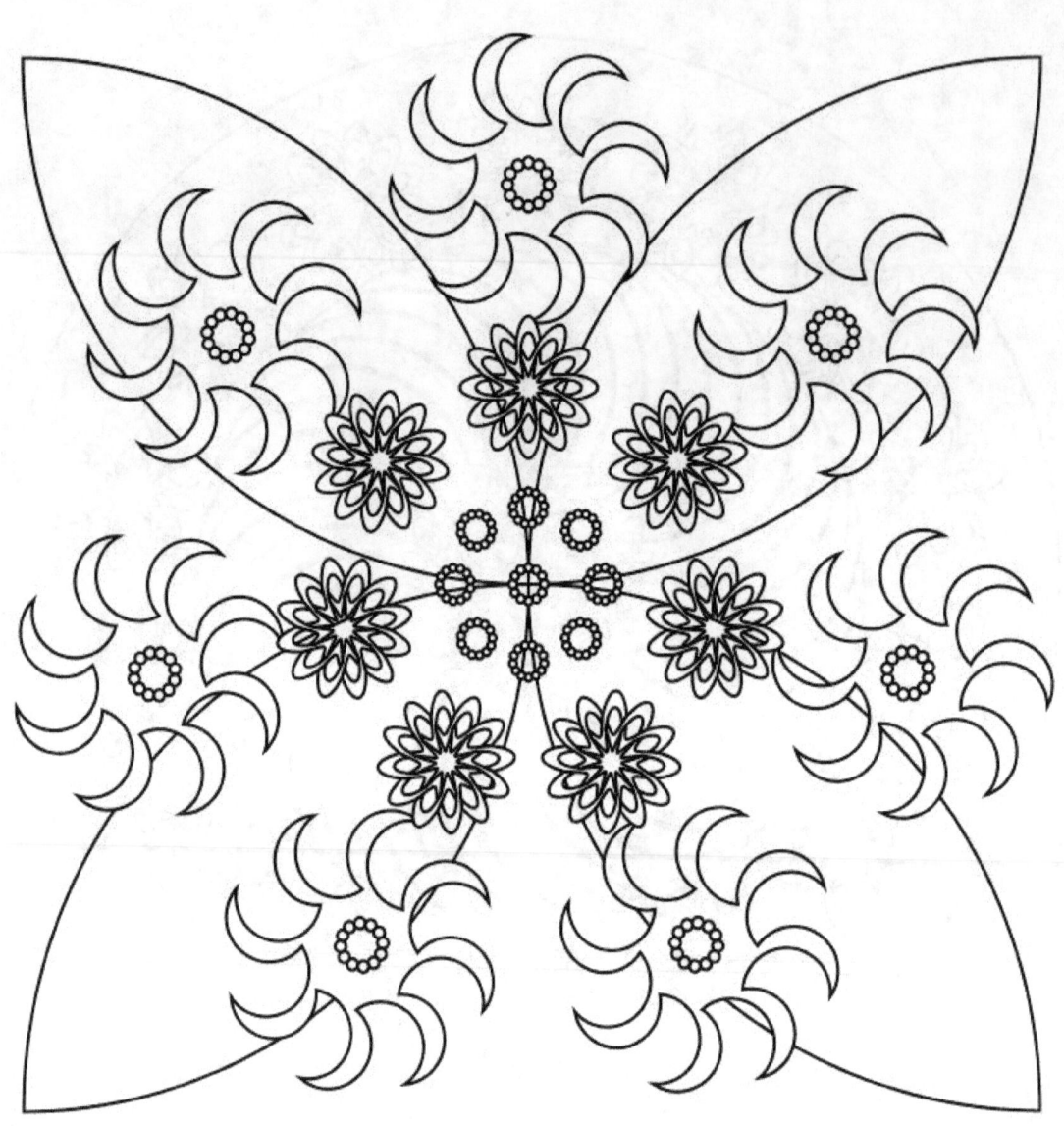

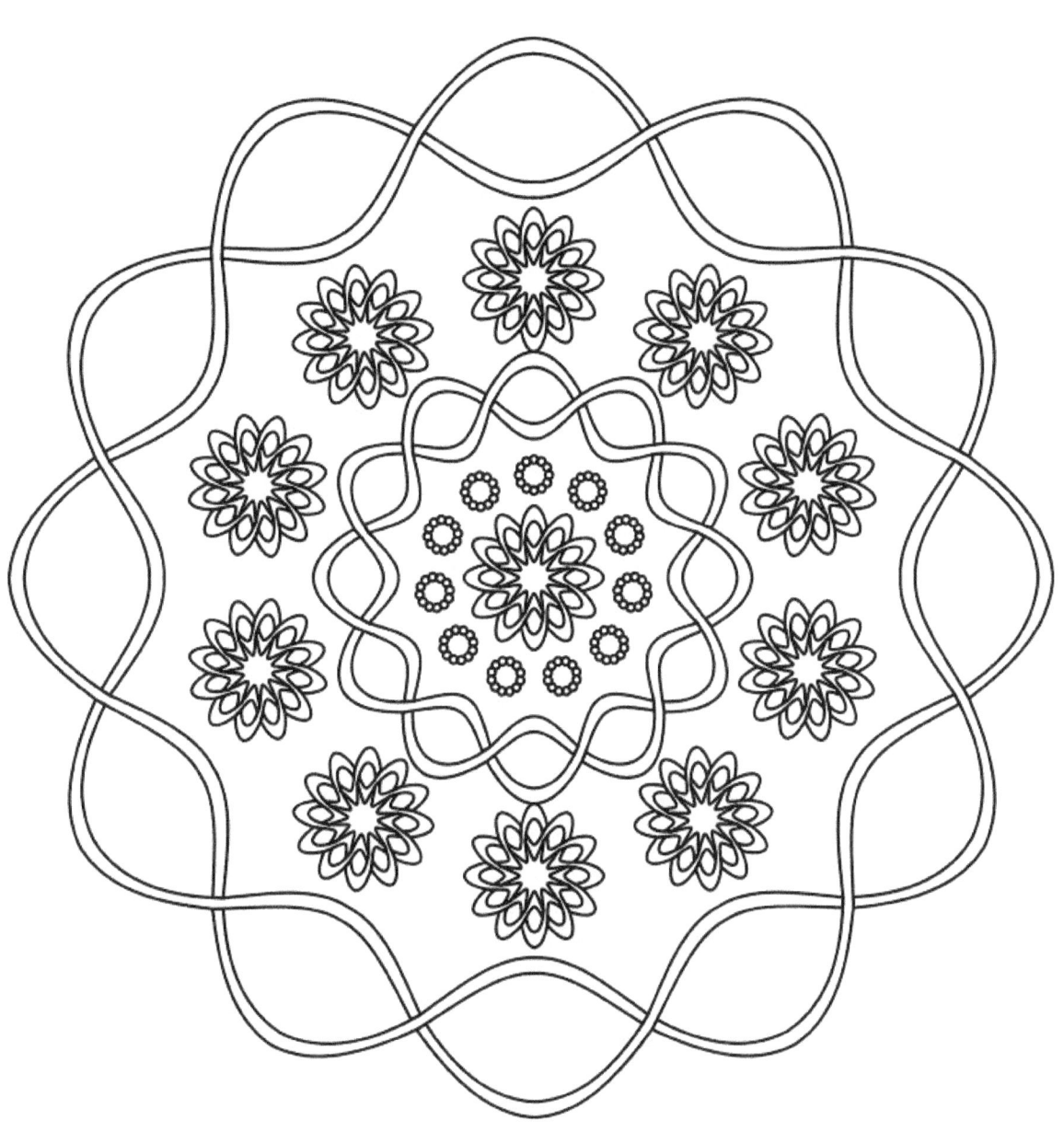

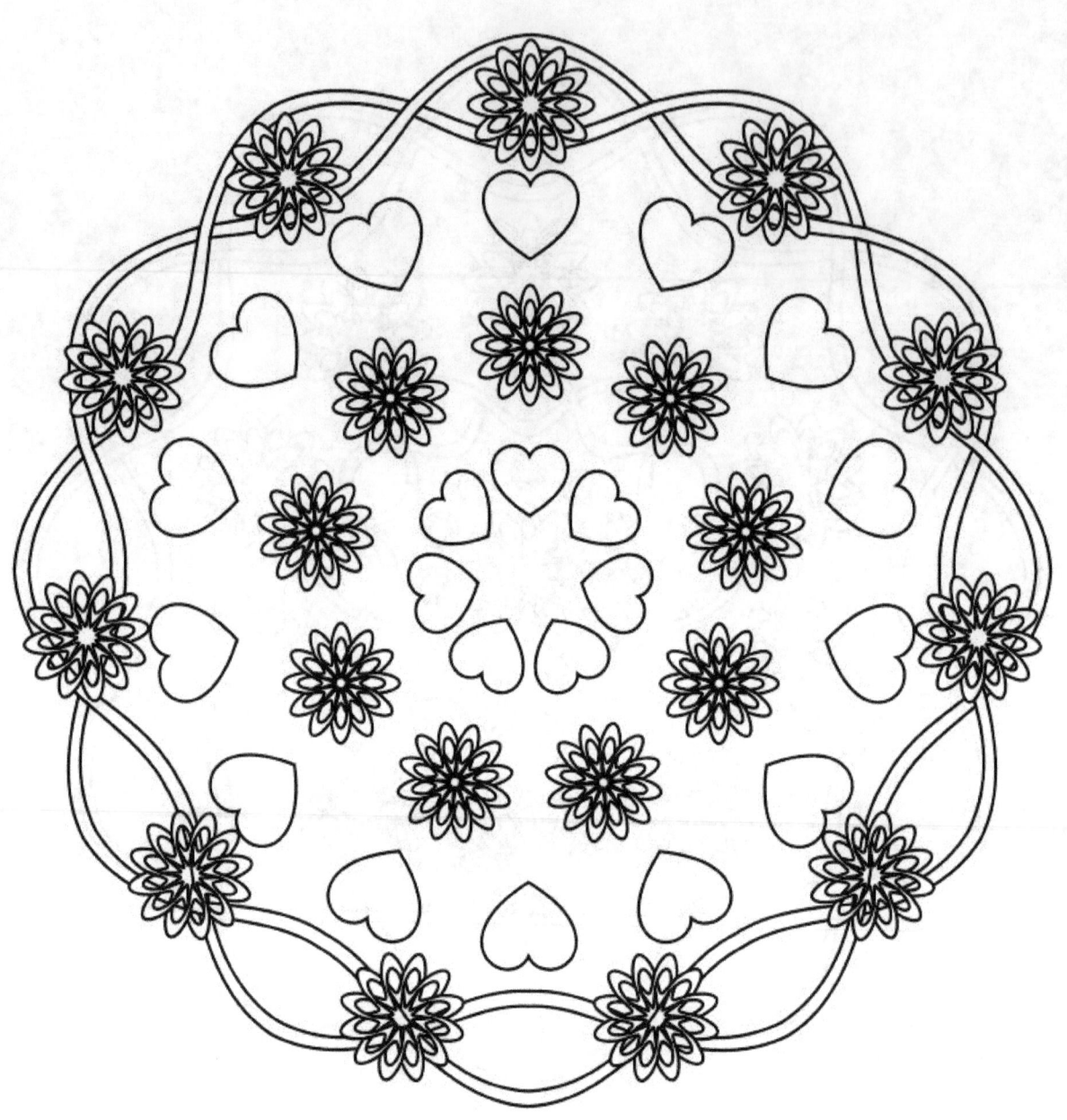

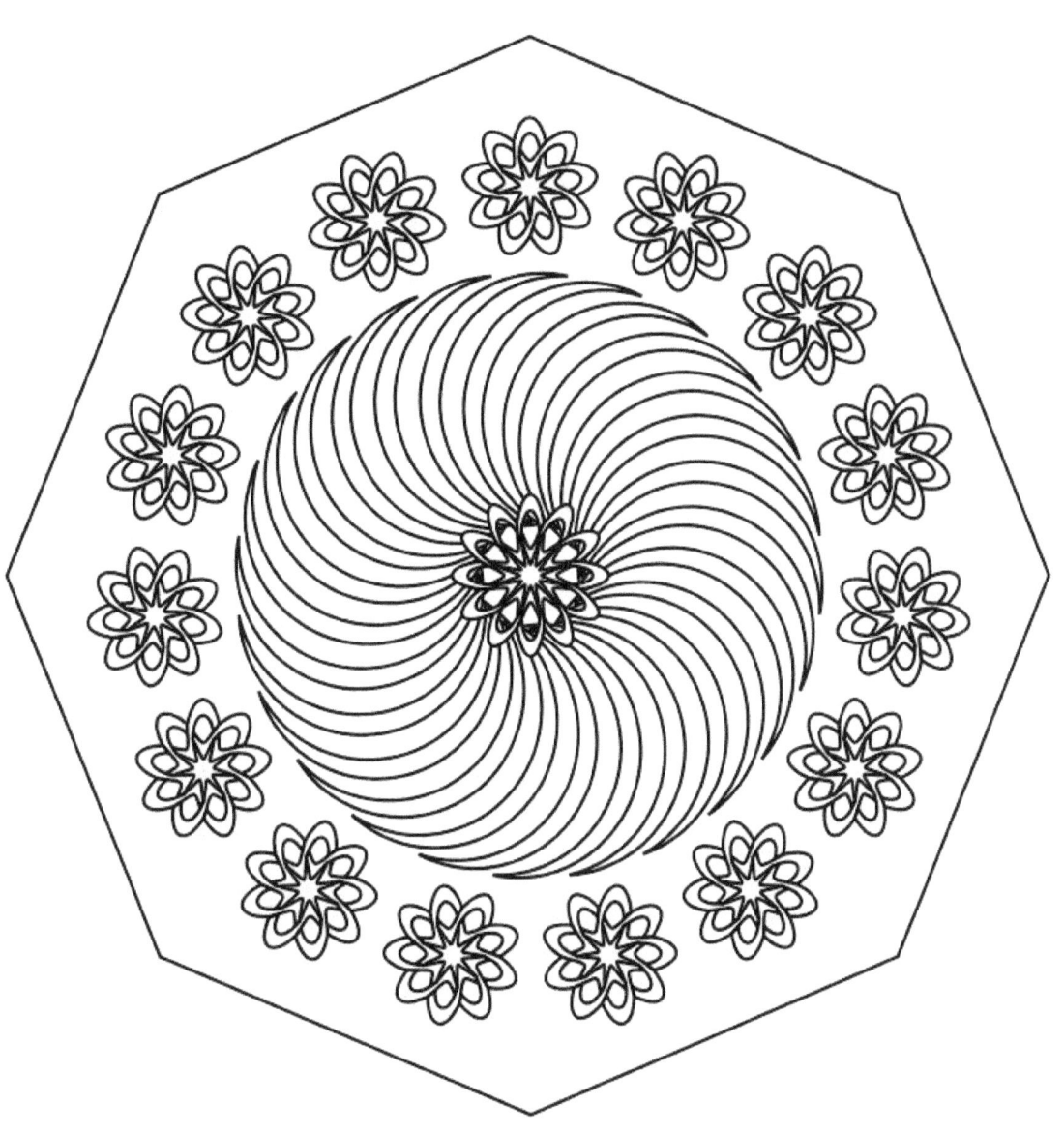

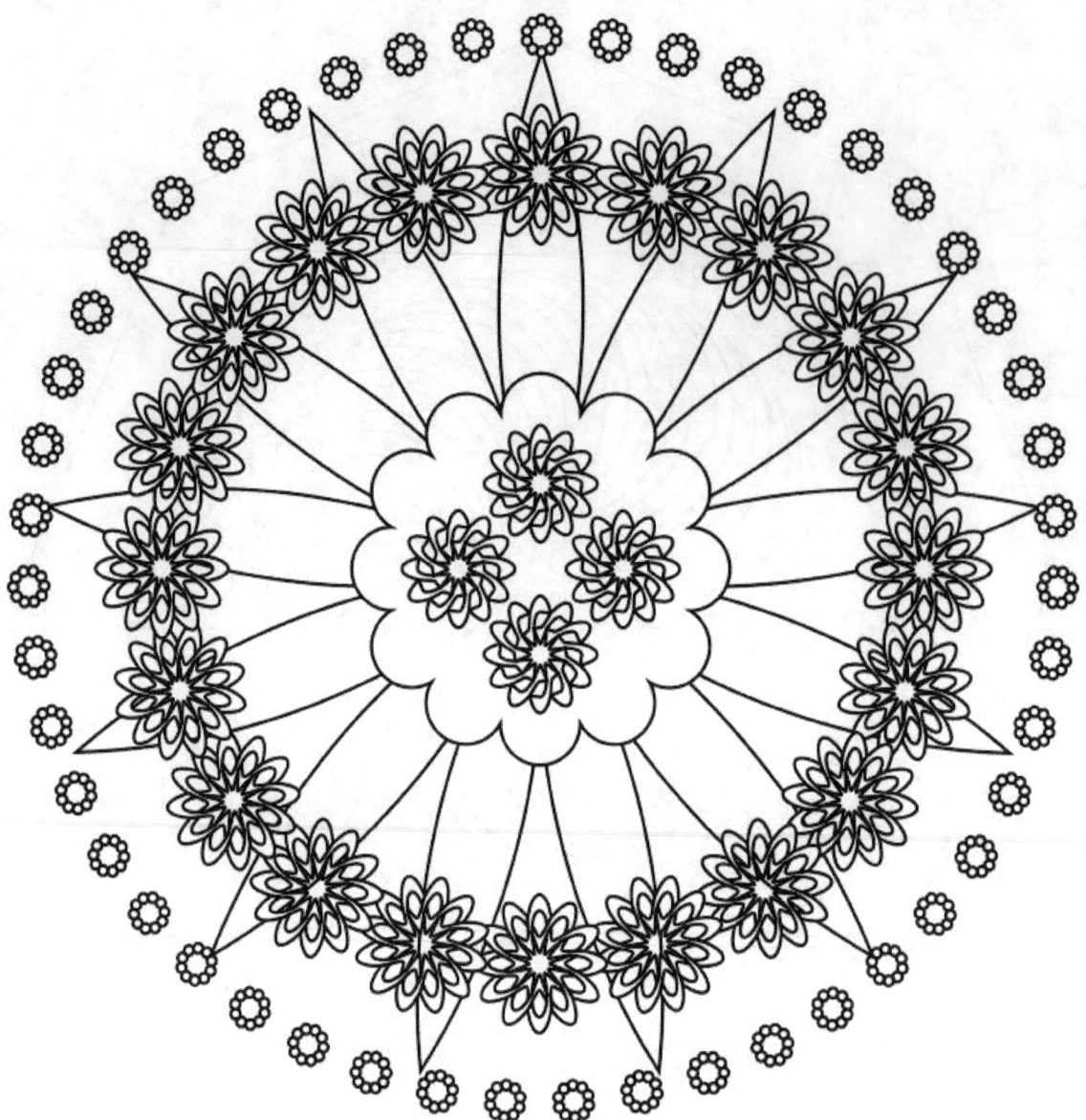

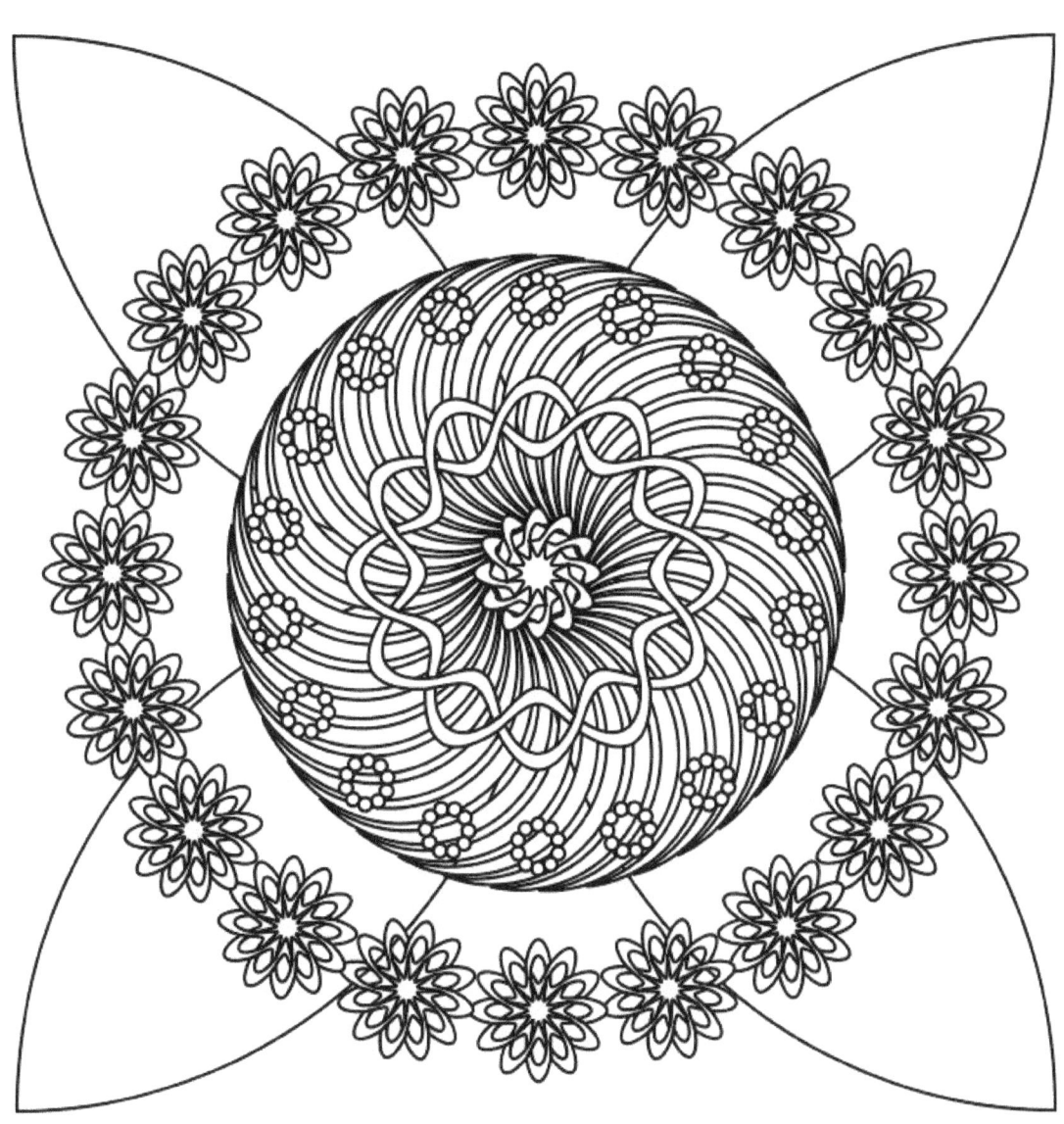

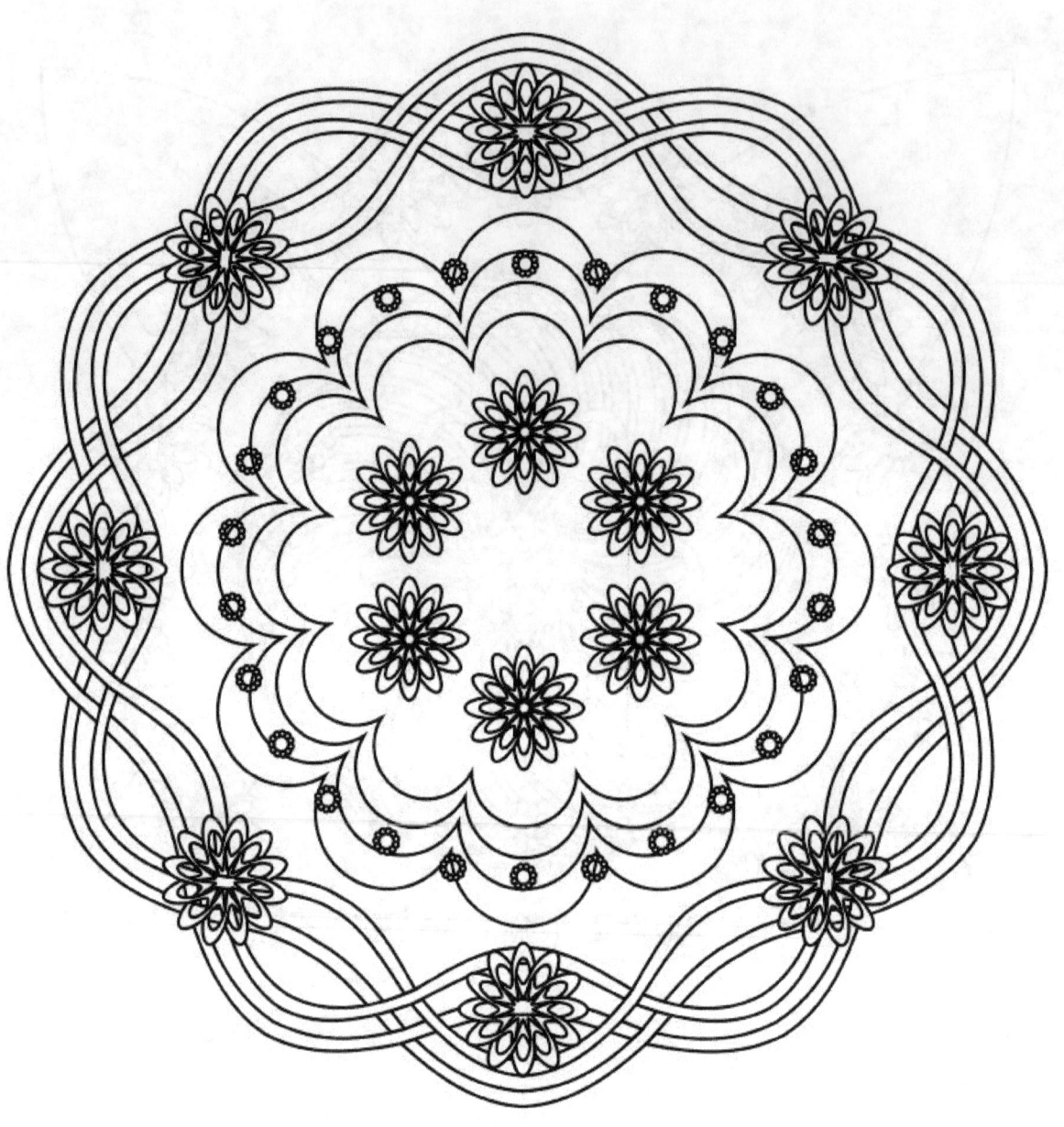

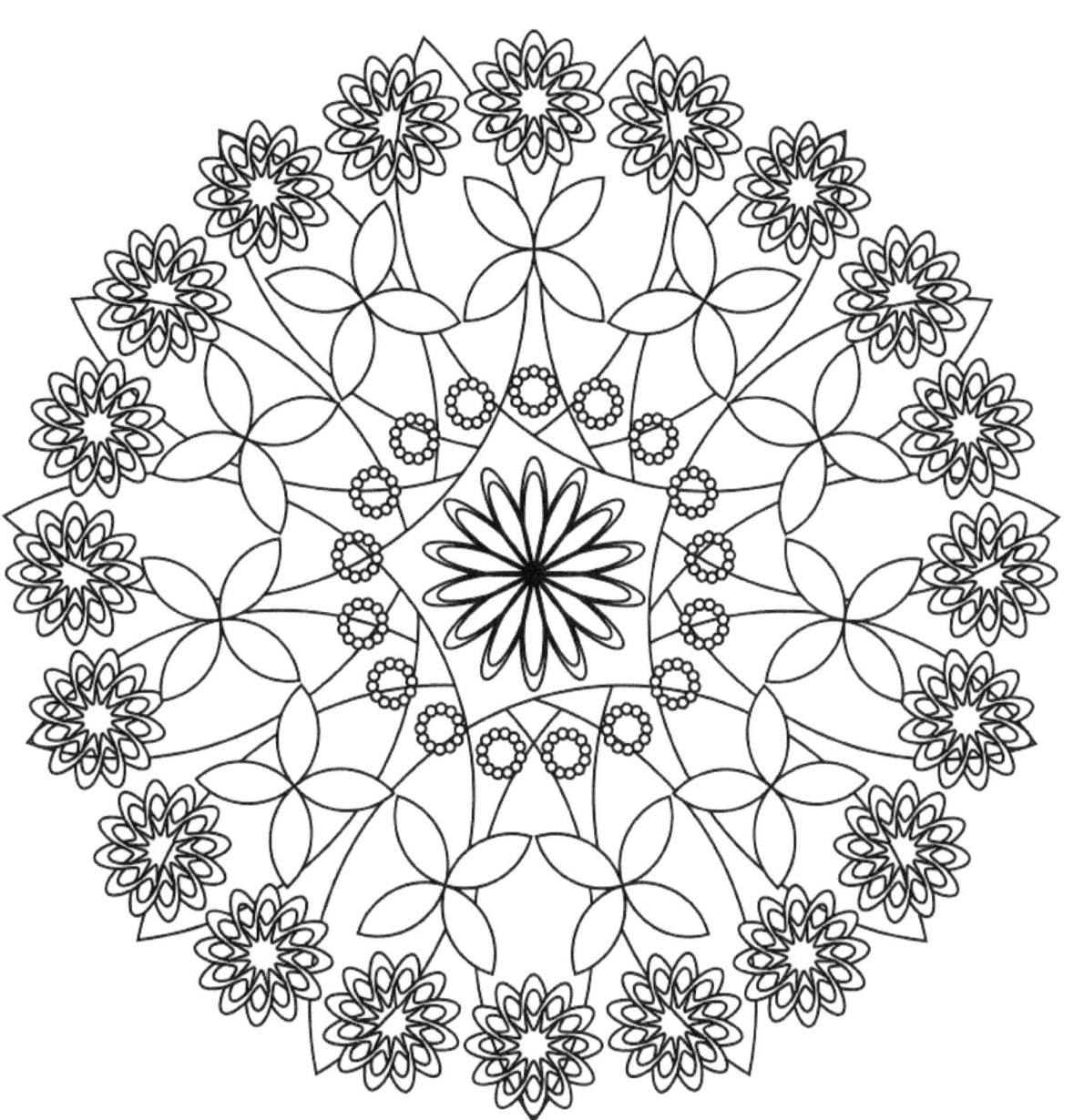

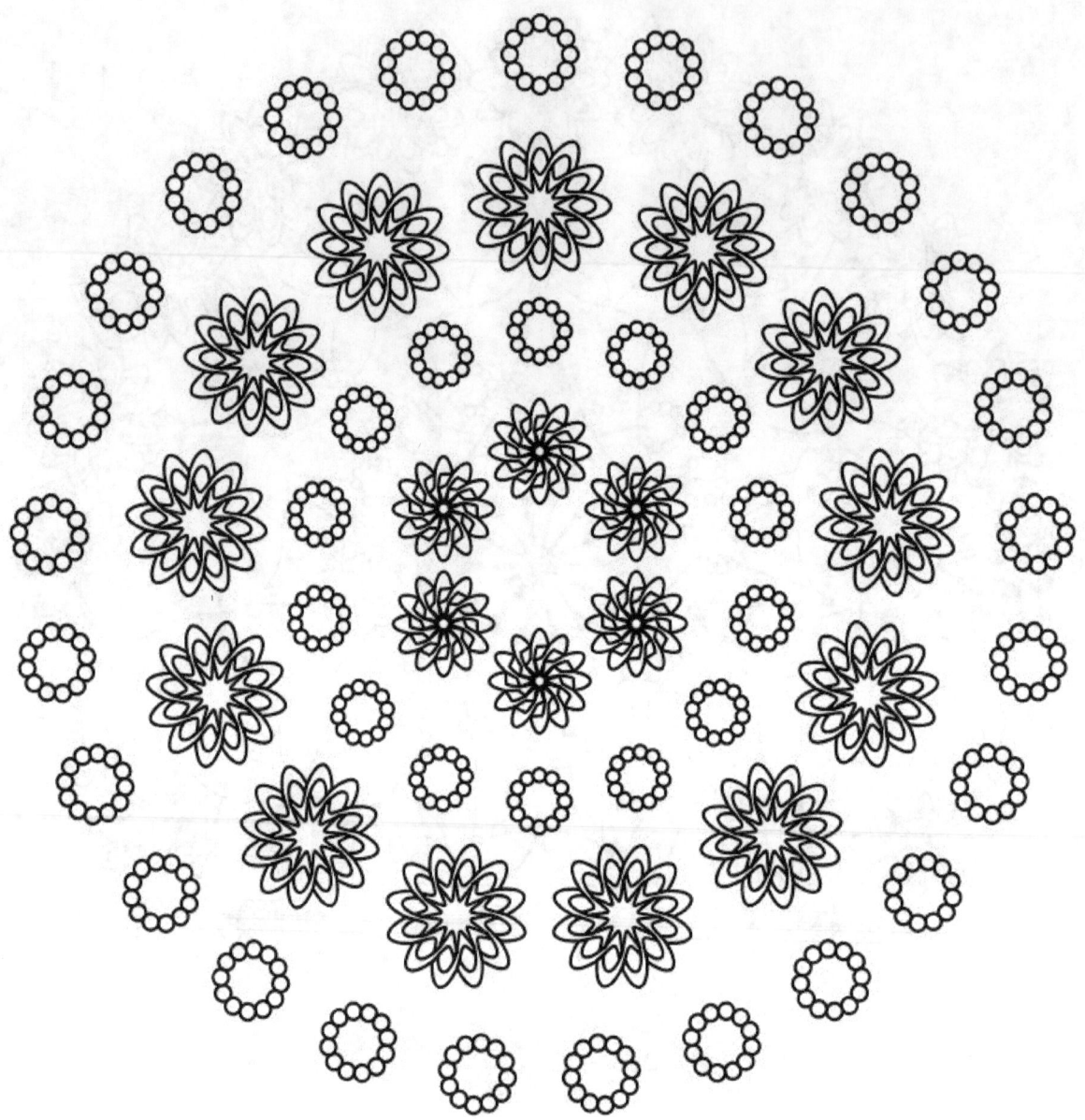

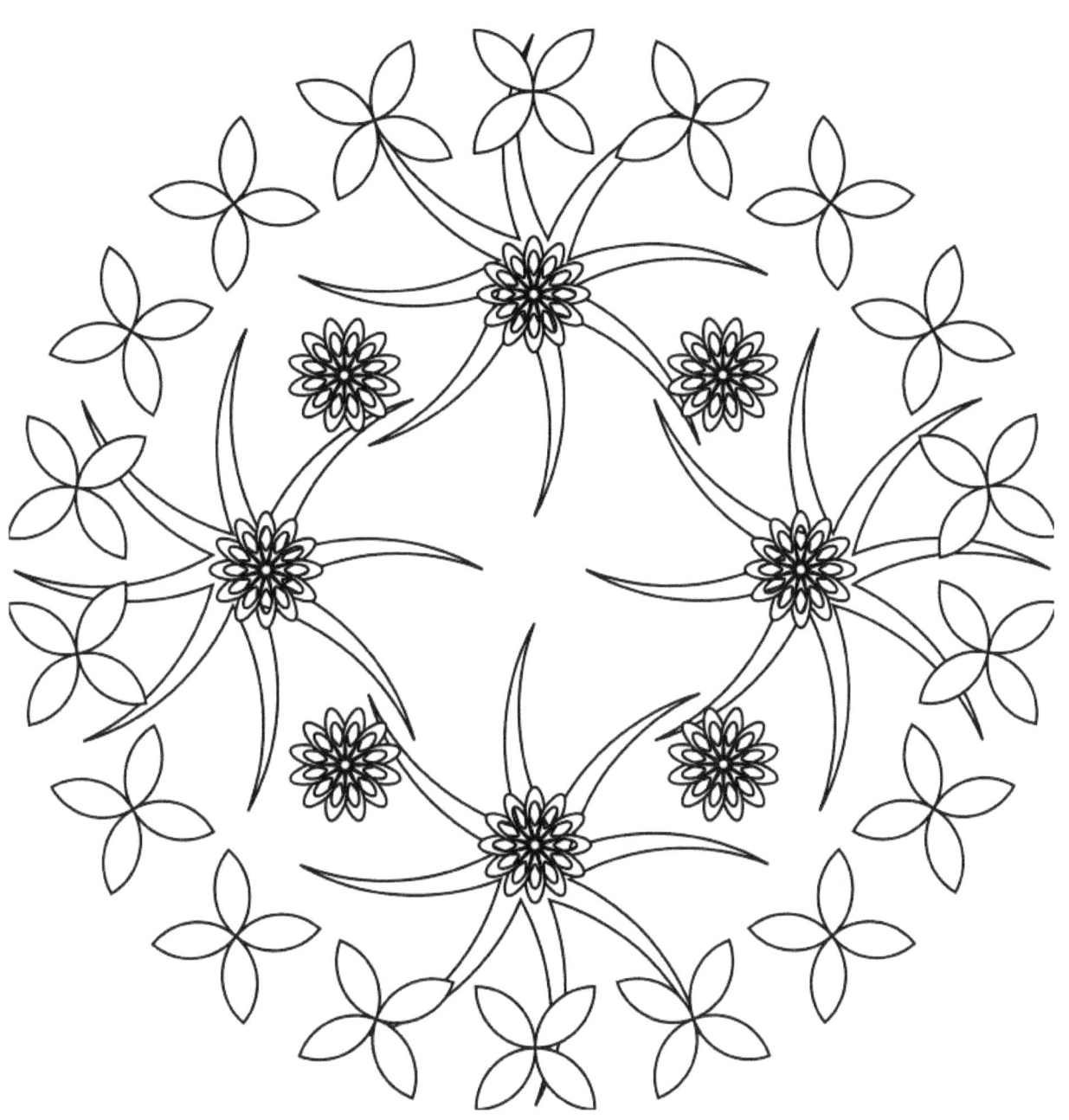

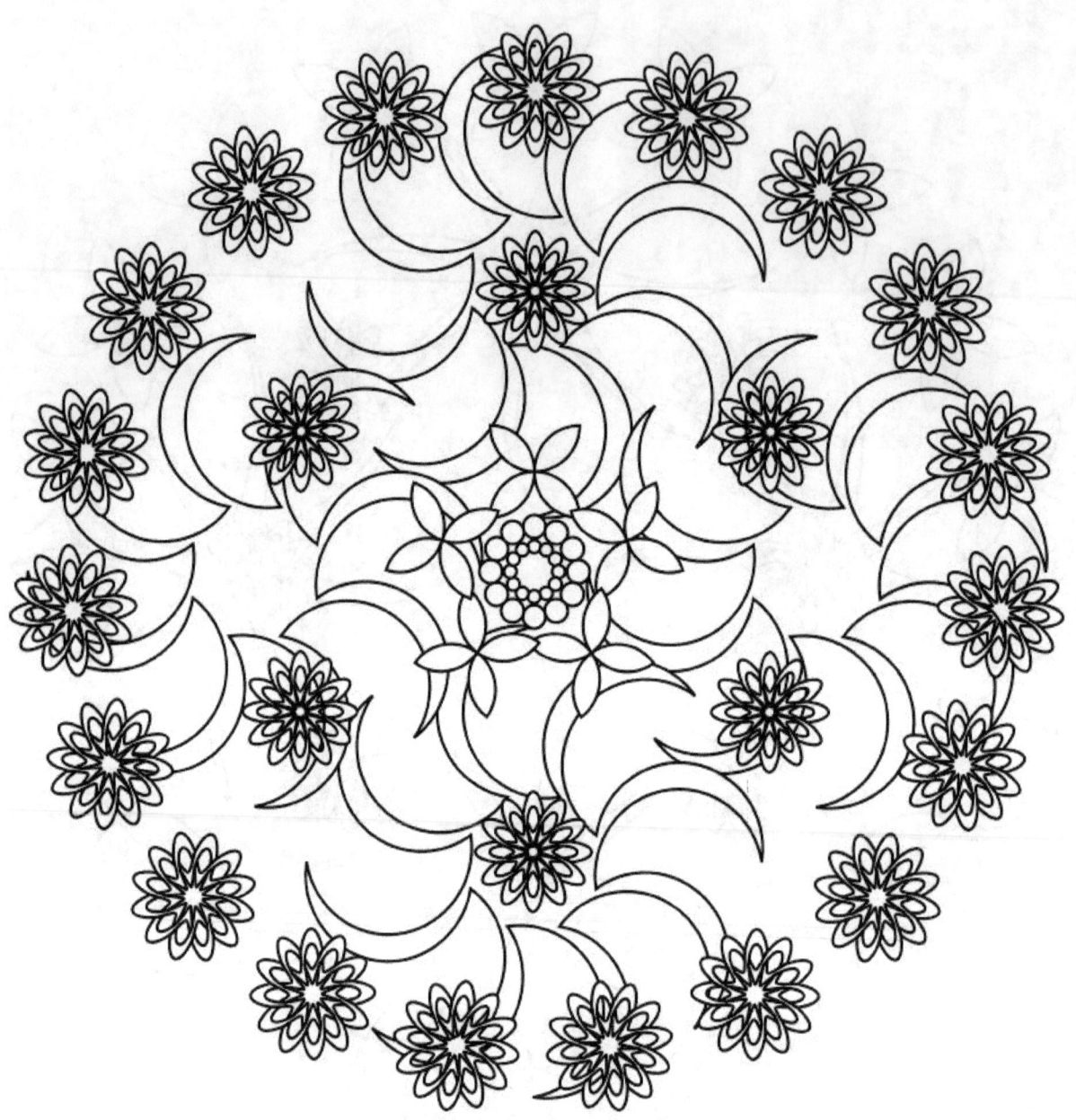

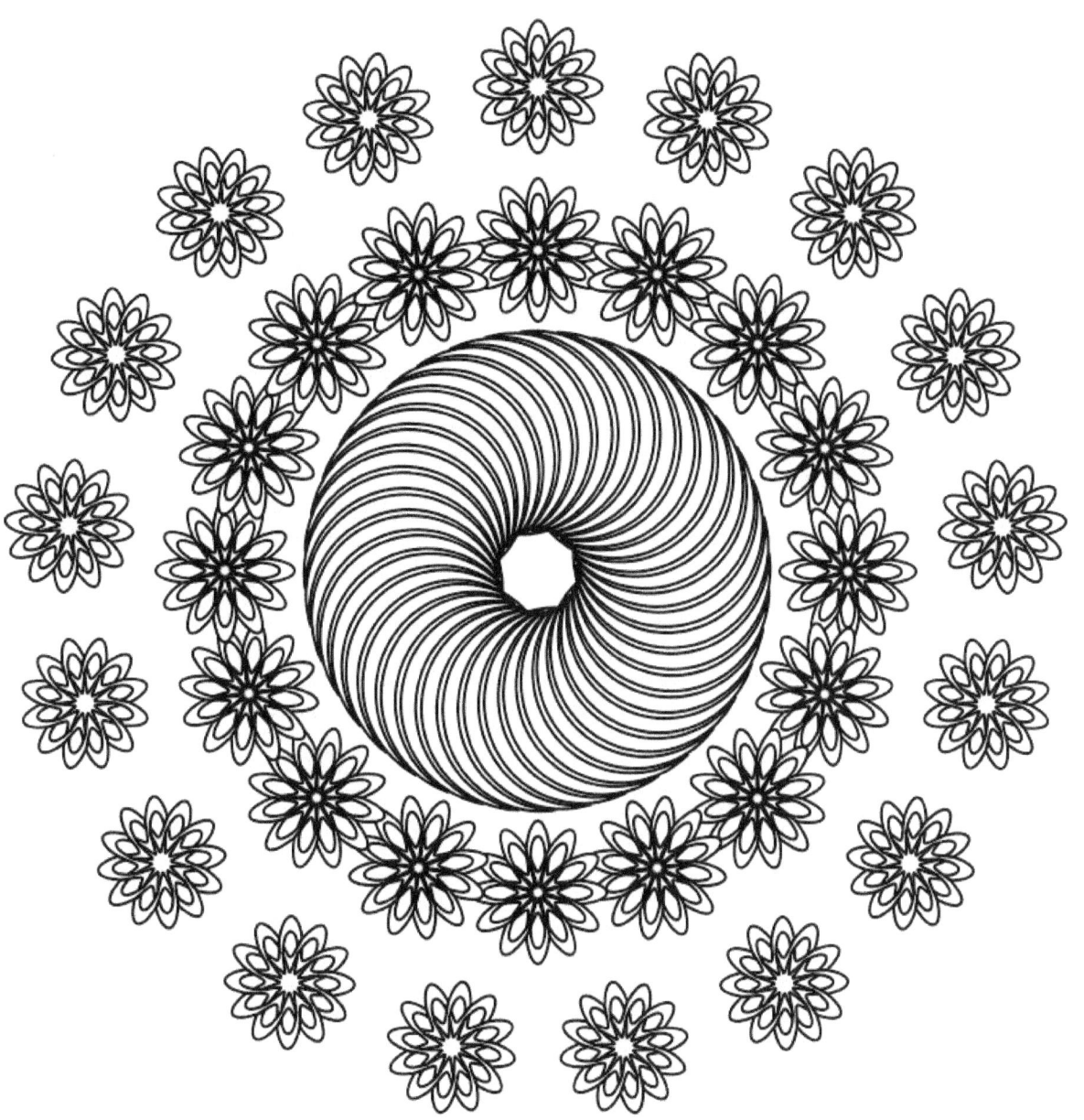

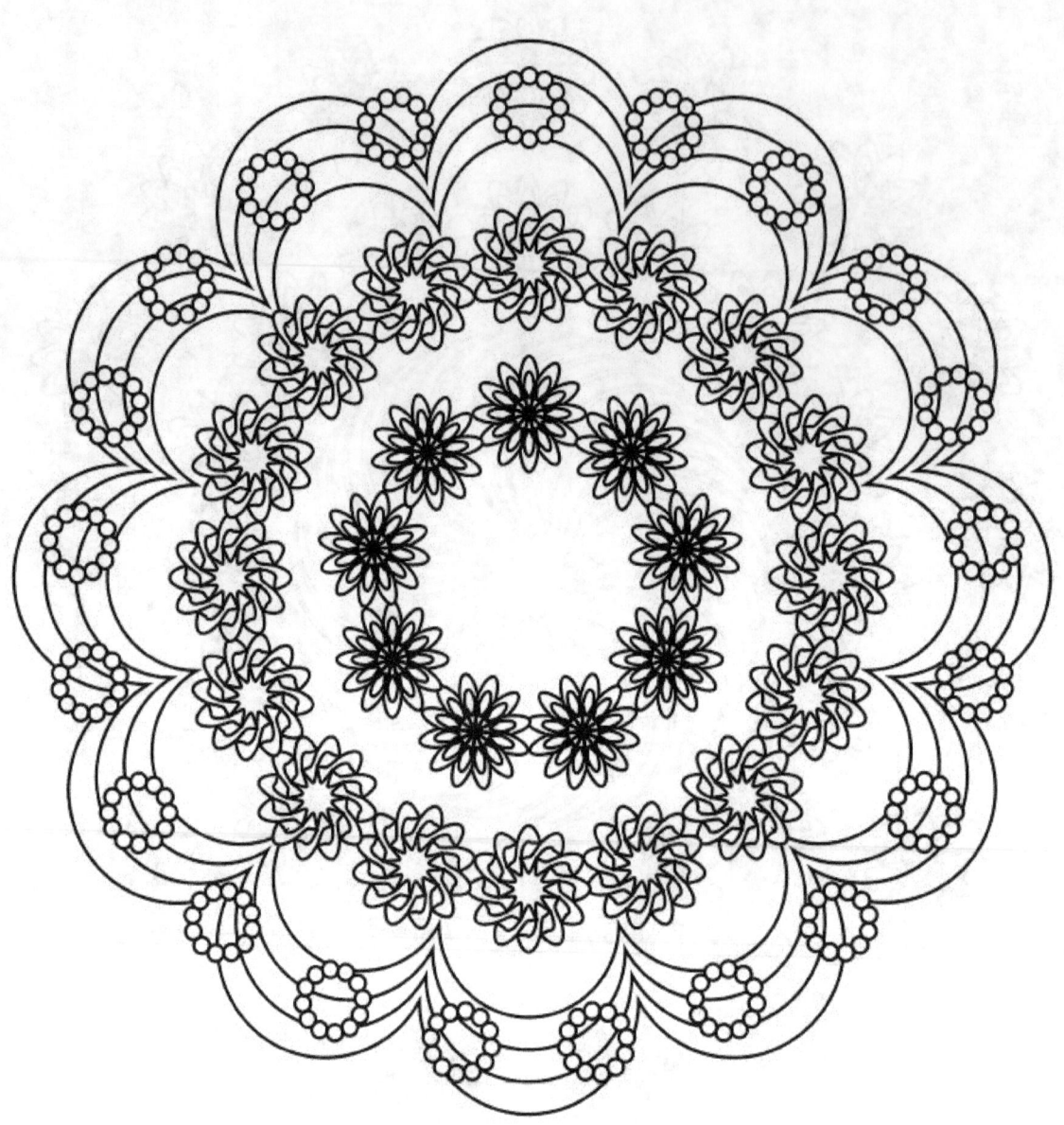

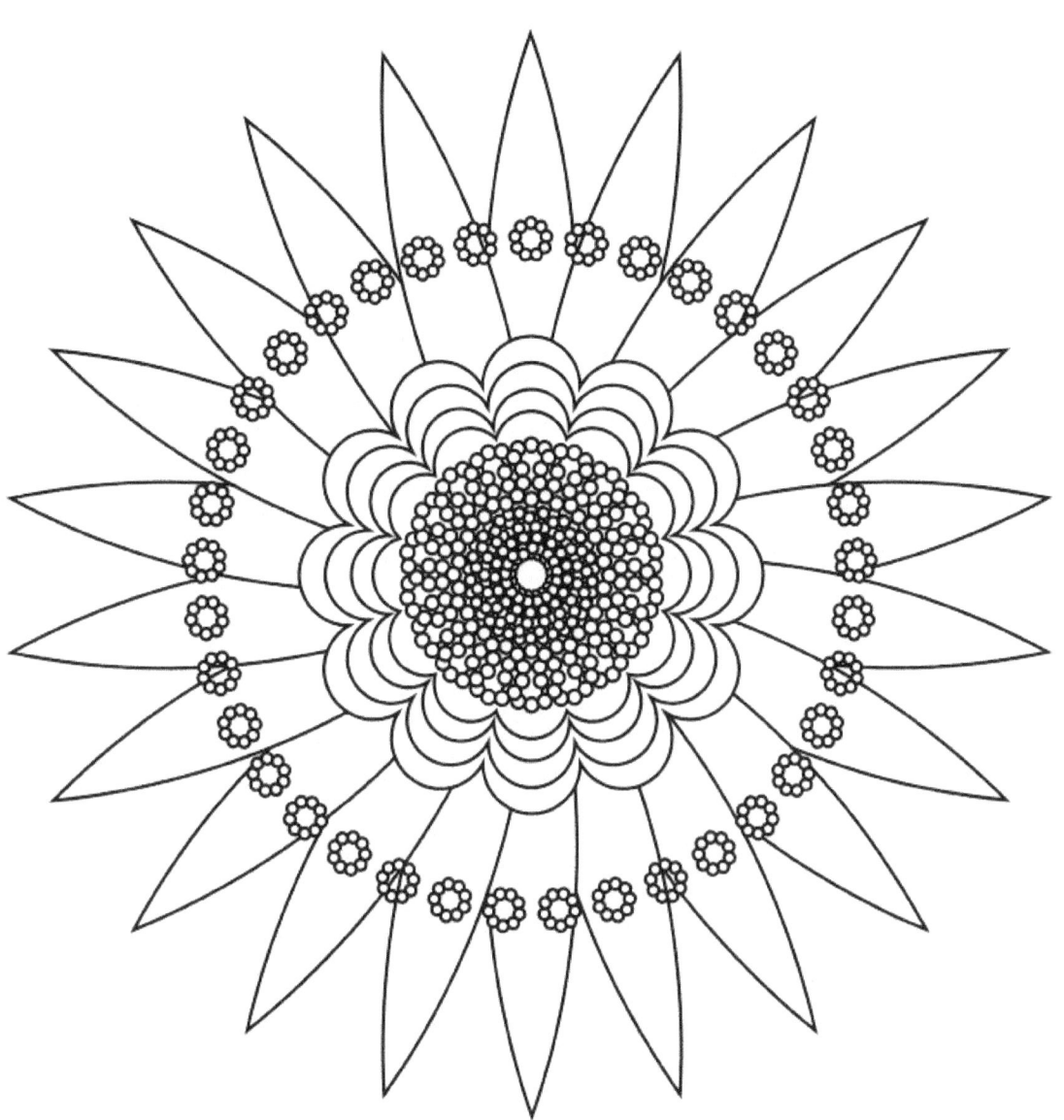

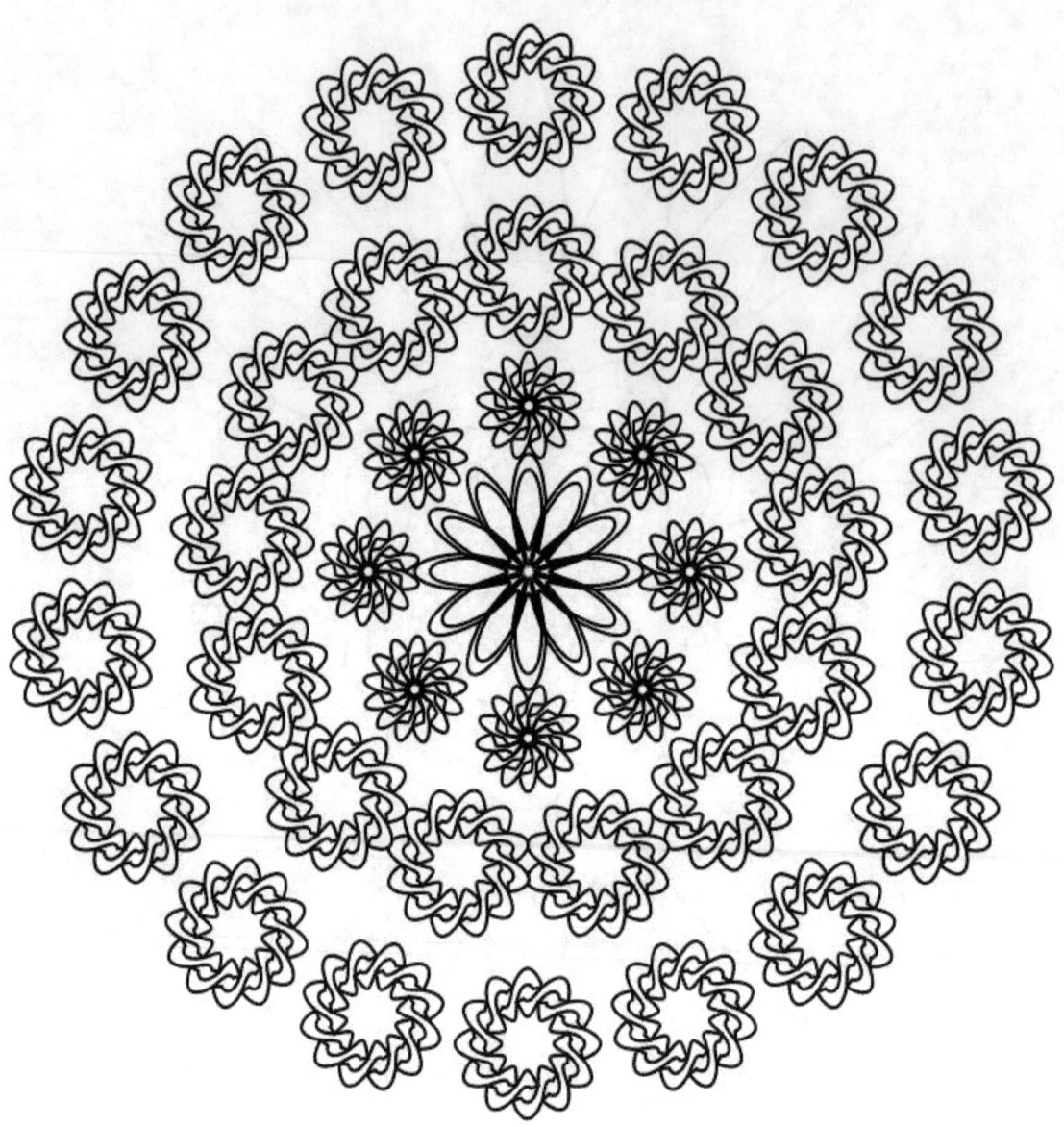

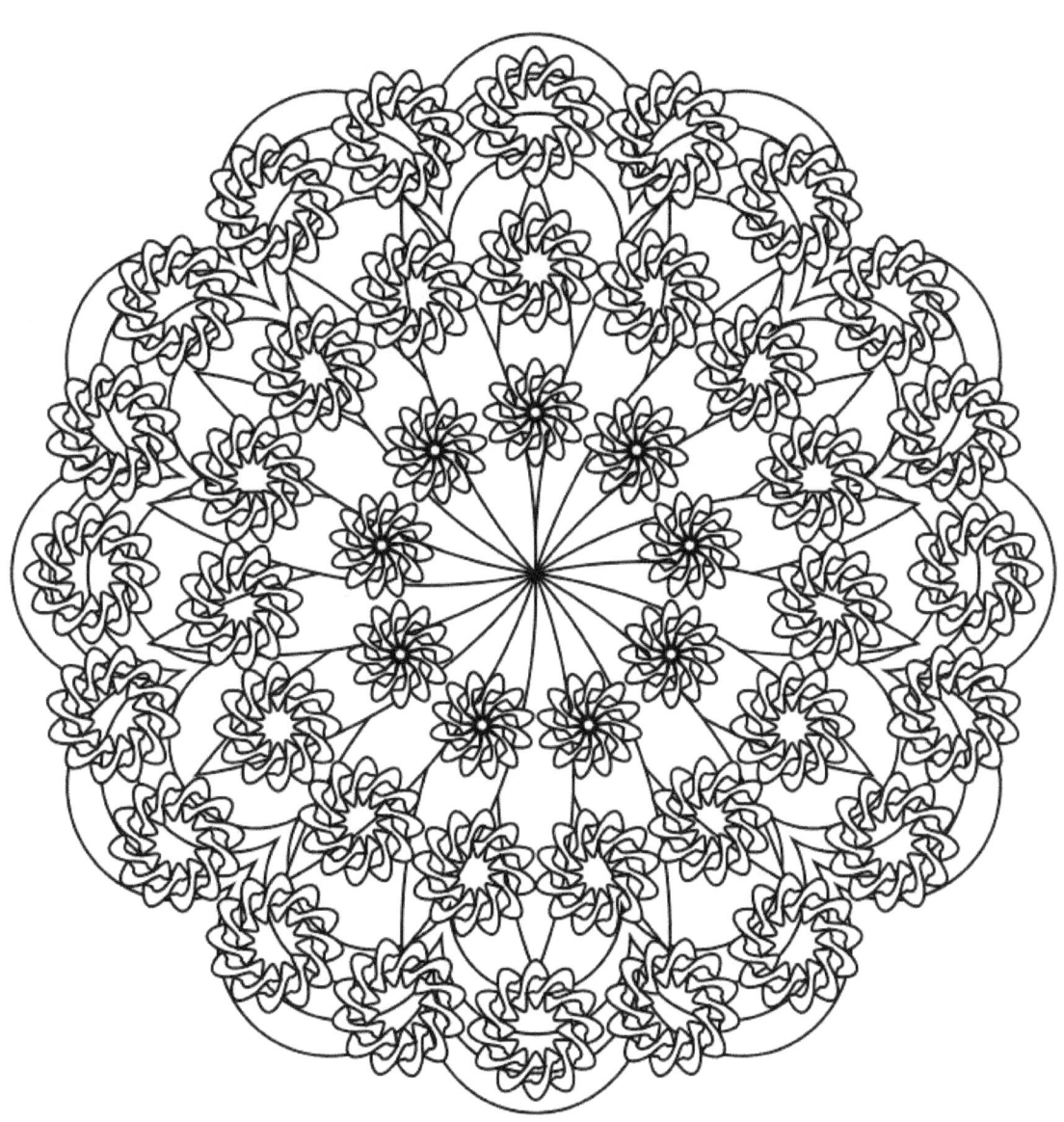

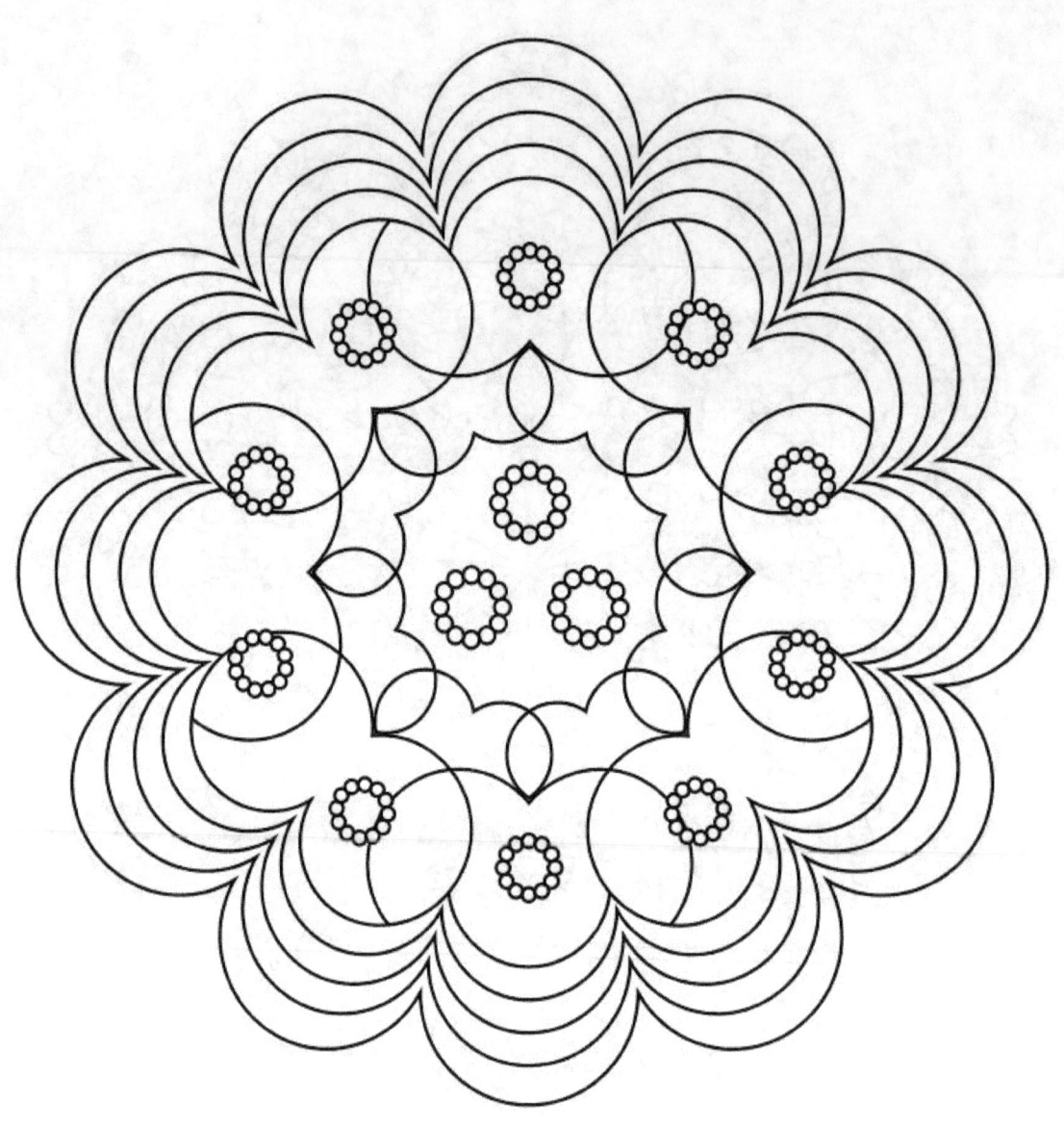